Living Through History

THE SECOND WORLD WAR

C.A.R. HILLS

Batsford Academic and Educational
London

ACKNOWLEDGMENTS

The Author and Publishers would like to thank the following for their kind permission to reproduce copyright material: Associated Press for figures 5 and 59; BBC TV for figure 49; Camera Press for figures 8 and 53; Marie S. Douglas for figure 17; Ruth Evans for figure 40 and extracts from Mathilde Wolff-Mönckeberg (ed. Ruth Evans), *On the Other Side*, Peter Owen Ltd, 1979; Mrs Fry for figure 44; Imperial War Museum for figures 1, 13, 14, 15, 16, 18, 21, 22, 23, 24, 25, 26, 42, 57, 58 and 60; Sir Osbert Lancaster and John Murray for figure 50; Mandel Archive for figure 41; Farley Mowat for extracts from *And No Birds Sang*, Anthony Mott, 1984; Novosti for figures 9, 10, 11, 12, 27, 28, 54, 55 and 56; Photosource for the frontispiece and figures 2, 3, 4, 6, 7, 19, 20, 29, 39, 46 and 47; Popperfoto for figures 30, 31, 32, 36, 43, 45 and 48; Photo Lapi-Viollet for figure 34; Photo Harlingue-Viollet for figure 35; William Younger for figure 51. The pictures were researched by Patricia Mandel.

Cover pictures
The colour photograph shows a queue outside a fishmonger's (Imperial War Museum); the portrait is of Noor Inayat Khan; the photograph on the right shows Japanese soldiers being taken prisoner by the Americans at Guadalcanal (Photosource).

Typeset by Tek-Art Ltd, West Wickham, Kent
Printed in Great Britain by
R.J. Acford Ltd
Chichester, Sussex
for the publishers
Batsford Academic and Educational,
an imprint of B.T. Batsford Ltd,
4 Fitzhardinge Street
London W1H 0AH

ISBN 0 7134 4531 9

CONTENTS

LIST OF ILLUSTRATIONS

THE SECOND WORLD WAR

The Second World War was the greatest and most devastating conflict in the history of mankind. Estimates of the number of people who died as a result of the conflict vary, but most put it between 50 and 60 million: a truly terrible figure of human suffering. Millions more were injured, many permanently. The material damage caused by the war was also enormous: cities all over Europe and Japan lay in ruins when the war ended in 1945; many countries (the Soviet Union, Poland, Yugoslavia, France) had their industrial resources cut by a half or two-thirds.

In the past, a war on such a scale would have taken decades, even centuries, to recover from. But, paradoxically, the results of this tremendous conflict are often hard to see today. In many of the countries most scarred by the fighting, the war years were followed by a huge upsurge of material prosperity and a rebuilding faster than seemed possible: it soon became difficult to recognize the former bomb-sites among the gleaming new structures of steel, glass and concrete. During the war, millions of men had become used to the idea of attempting to kill other men they did not know, and many were forced, by being soldiers, to take part in acts of cruelty; but, this duty done, they usually went back to living normal and peaceful lives. To their children and grandchildren, their wartime experience had taken place in a different world. So this war, so recent as it is, seems to have receded into the distant past: perhaps only when we meet those whose bodies or minds are still damaged by the conflict do we realize how close it is.

During this war, the human capacity for cruelty, which people had thought forgotten in the civilized twentieth century, reached a new and fearful peak. To take only what seem the worst examples of suffering, the barbarities inflicted on the Jews and Gypsies in the Nazi extermination camps or the experience of the helpless citizens of Hiroshima and Nagasaki who suffered the atom bomb hardly bear thinking about. Yet it is also true that the war was a release of human potential for living intensely, a chance for ordinary people to have richer emotions and experience than they had had before. In that era, for instance, there was very little travel abroad for the majority; the war transported millions to far-off countries of which they had barely heard, providing the most exciting interlude in lives that perhaps seem rather limited compared with the opportunities available today.

At first, the nations went to war unwillingly, with little of the popular enthusiasm that had marked the outbreak of the First World War, and with people patiently waiting their turn to be called up rather than flocking to the colours. But then, people who had previously felt they were only "cogs in the wheel" found that their endurance, their courage, their ingenuity were suddenly called for: their countries needed them. It has been said that wars have a tendency to throw up interesting characters, but it would perhaps be truer to say that they *allow* people to become interesting: in this war many a man or woman, whose name would otherwise be entirely unknown to history, emerged suddenly to play a herioc, tragic or villainous part, and then often disappeared back into the obscurity from which he or she came. In this book we shall look at the careers of several men and women whom the war allowed to become extraordinary in this way.

And it was a tremendous drama into which people emerged: a war with raging dictators such as Hitler; great, popular, democratic leaders such as Churchill; sudden and devastating reversals of fortune as the war rolled through continent after continent; heroism and disaster. The great events of the war – the doomed uprising of the Jews against the Nazis in the Warsaw Ghetto, the tragic attempt at an airborne landing at Arnhem in September 1944, or the final suicide of Hitler in his bunker as the Russians fought their way into his devastated capital, Berlin – are tragic or symbolic dramas which still fascinate us.

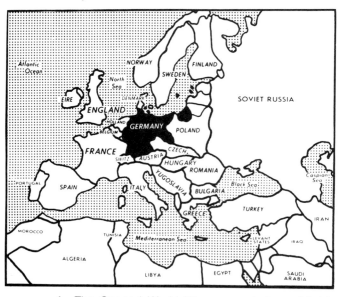

1 The Second World War was a truly worldwide conflict: German-occupied territory (*above*) in 1938; (*below*) in 1941.

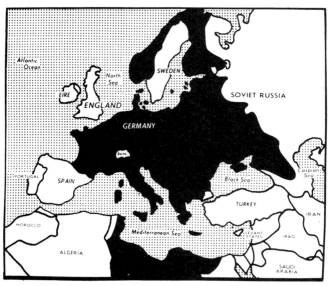

The Second World War was the first truly worldwide conflict. The First World War had been called a "world war", and indeed fighting took part in many parts of the world, but the conflicts outside Europe were sideshows, and within Europe itself the decisive field of action was a narrow strip of north-eastern France and Belgium. The Second World War was entirely different: by 1942, three years after war had broken out in Europe, war was being waged fully in all continents except the two Americas, and men from these two continents were involved in the conflict – even from remote South America. It was Brazilian troops fighting for the Allies who took Turin in northern Italy from the Germans in April 1945. Although there was fighting all over the world, there were four great land theatres: western Europe, Russia, the Middle East and North Africa and the Far East, and men from each continent swarmed across all the others. Indians fought for the British Empire in North and Central Africa, Canadians launched attacks on Normandy in northern France, and in 1945 New Zealanders were holding the peace between Italians and Yugoslavs over the disputed city of Trieste.

The war came to have this exceptionally complex, worldwide character because it was not really one large war, but a series of large and small wars which gradually coalesced into one huge one. The war is usually dated as having happened between 1939 and 1945, but this is only really true of the war in Europe (and does not even apply to Soviet Russia). For other parts of the world the war may have started earlier, started later, finished earlier, or gone on long after 1945 and what the world called "peace". In Vietnam, for instance, a terrible war had its roots in the events of the Second World War and went on for another 30 years, until the Communists established their domination of the whole country in 1975.

Faced with trying to understand all these diverse wars – the war between China and Japan, the Chinese civil war, the Greek and Yugoslav civil wars – all of which became involved in the larger conflict, is there any larger pattern which we can see? There were two large wars, in fact, which enveloped all the others, and each seems to have been caused, at least partly, by the ambitions of an aggressive power. In Europe, the Nazi dictator Hitler came to power in Germany in 1933 with a programme to overturn the results of the First World War, which Germany had lost, and a long-term plan to build up a racial empire in eastern Europe at the expense of peoples Hitler considered subhuman. In the Far East, Japan embarked, in 1931, on a programme of conquering her great but enfeebled neighbour China and also on a larger-scale programme of domination in south-east Asia and the Pacific which was to bring her into conflict with the United States. These two ambitious powers, Germany and Japan, came into loose alliance as the Axis (and brought in the lesser power of Italy); by 1941, there were ranged against them the Allies – Soviet Russia, the United States and Britain with her empire. Other powers by this time were either conquered by or uneasy allies of one side or the other.

Because the war brought the application of science and technology to fighting on an undreamt-of scale, it was ultimately great economic power and resources that counted: and, in taking on such an alliance as the Soviet Union, the United States and Britain, Germany and Japan had brought upon themselves a force that must ultimately destroy them. This, on the face of it, seems an act of madness, and we must ask why these powers acted in this way. This leads to the whole question of how the war originated, which has been endlessly debated by historians. However, what seems likely is that, initially at least, Germany and Japan had limited aims. Germany hoped to conquer eastern Europe and Russia; Japan wanted to take over China and south-east Asia. If they had been able to stop at this, they might have been successful, or they might not. They thought they could gradually steal forward in a series of small conquests until they had achieved their respective empires, but eventually circumstances tempted them into declaring war on other world powers. By the time Germany declared war on the United States in December 1941, Hitler may have become unbalanced, and he also believed he

2 Smiling British troops wave a farewell to women and babies as they set off on the road for France.

had an obligation to come in to support his ally Japan. For her part, Japan attacked America because she believed conflict with America was inevitable, and as she was weaker, she should get in the decisive blow first.

When the great powers came together in these great alliances, they still did not co-operate fully. Germany had come into war to support Japan, but that was about as far as their collaboration went. Fighting in the various theatres of action was carried out by different allies almost independently of each other. In Europe, after initial conquests by Germany of Poland in 1939 and France in 1940, the greatest battle by far was on the eastern front: the war between Germany and Soviet Russia. Russia did almost no fighting against other powers during the war, while three-quarters of the entire German army was usually engaged fighting Russia. This was the war's most savage conflict, and probably the decisive one. From 1940 to 1944 it was virtually the only European conflict: from 1940 almost all Europe was under Hitler's domination. Only when the Allies landed in Normandy in June 1944 did Germany have to fight a western front as well as an eastern one.

For those four years, Britain had to face the dilemma of being at war with Germany without being able to fight her, and this led Britain into concentrating on a war in North

3 The result of an air attack on houses in London. Until 1942 a wife was more likely to be killed in a bombing raid than her husband was to be killed at the front.

Africa, first largely against Italy, and then when she grew weak, against the Germans. With North Africa conquered in 1943, British attention switched to the forces slowly fighting their way up the heel of Italy, mainly against the Germans, and this process was still not over when the war ended two years later.

In the Far East, Japan had mainly been attempting to conquer China since 1931, but from 1938-45 this conflict seemed virtually suspended. Japan made conquests in south-east Asia which drew her into conflict with Britain in such countries as Burma, but the main Far Eastern war was between Japan and the United States from December 1941, and this was fought not in south-east Asia but amid the islands of the Pacific Ocean; Japan's control of her land empire was still substantially intact when she was decisively defeated in the Pacific. Another vital battle was fought for control of the Atlantic by

4 The human capacity for cruelty reached a new and fearful peak: prisoners separated by barbed wire in a Nazi concentration camp.

means of U-boats: Germany, Britain and the States were the main powers involved in this.

These were the main wars: there were others – Ethiopia, skirmishing in the Caribbean – and they were important, but really sideshows compared with the great wars.

As well as being a truly worldwide war, the war was also fought by every conceivable method and in all dimensions, as science was brought in as never before to serve the needs of conflict. The scientific achievements and discoveries directly connected with the war, and the technical breakthroughs – radar, rocket-guided missiles, modern code-breaking as practised by Britain's ULTRA – were immensely important, and new weapons abounded: aircraft carriers, the full use of tanks, the anti-tank gun, the German "smoke thrower" (*Nebelwerfer*), aircraft used for mass bombing of civilians. But the conflict remained largely a traditional one with masses of men fighting their way across country as they had always done; landing craft, jeeps and trucks were also among the decisive weapons. In Europe, the war ended in a traditional way with the three great Allies eventually meeting on German territory in May 1945 after Hitler commited suicide in his underground bunker. But in the Far East the war ended with the most advanced and terrible application of technology yet: the harnessing of nuclear power to drop two atom bombs on Japan. By taking technology to a level where it could potentially threaten the survival of the whole human race, we had perhaps ensured that, as well as being the greatest of the traditional type of conflict, where large masses of soldiers and civilians become involved for a number of years in personal war efforts, the Second World War would also be the last of its kind.

In this book we shall approach the war by looking at the experience of people who waged it and had to endure it. With such a huge and diverse war, we cannot hope to look at all

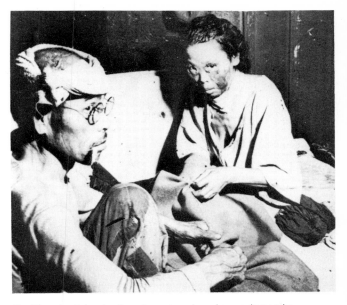

5 The decision to drop two atom bombs on Japan in 1945 brought the war to a swift end, but with what consequences?

different experiences or at people from a majority of the countries involved, but we will try to look at people who had the major *kinds* of experience: from fighting on foot or in the tanks to undergoing mass bombing to being a prisoner in the extermination camps to being a child in wartime. Some of the stories we will look at will be sad, and almost all will involve some hardship, but it is important, and can be inspiring, to understand such things. As the English historian Guy Wint has put it:

It is clear that, to the many millions who fought and suffered unvocally, to the ignorant armies clashing by night, unselfconsciously those who survived owe an inexpiable debt. It seems, at some points in history, that only through a convulsion involving millions is understanding painfully acquired. "The cut worm forgives the plough," said the poet Blake. By invoking this kind of charity, there can perhaps be forgiveness for the ungovernable fury of the instruments by which history is made. (Peter Calvocoressi and Guy Wint, *Total War*)

LEADERS

The twentieth century has been called the century of the common man, in contrast to the nineteenth with its cult of great leaders. Yet, the Second World War was a time of great political leaders with immense power. In four of the five major combatant nations there was a single, immensely influential leader who made most of the important decisions personally: Hitler in Germany, Stalin in the Soviet Union, Roosevelt in the United States of America, Churchill in Britain. Only in Japan was there no single, dominant leader figure, perhaps because of the country's distinctive political system. In Italy there was another all-powerful leader, Mussolini, a little less impressive, perhaps, than the other four. The four great leaders were intensely colourful and inspiring figures who commanded devotion from their peoples. Stalin and Hitler were dictators, leading the Communist and National Socialist (Nazi) parties in their respective countries. Roosevelt and Churchill co-existed with democratic systems but usually got their own way, although sometimes by argument and not command.

At a rather lower level, the war also gave rise to many more great political leaders who were important representatives of their own countries: Charles de Gaulle in France, Marshal Tito in Yugoslavia, Emperor Haile Selassie in Ethiopia. These men had the breadth of vision of great world leaders, and no doubt would have played a more important role if they had happened to be the representatives of larger countries.

Compared to the great political leaders, the military leaders and generals of the war seem colourless considered as a group, and they were certainly less important. The great political leaders were also commanders-in-chief who ran the war themselves. They dismissed any generals who disagreed with them: Stalin got rid of them by the score, and sometimes shot them for incompetence; Hitler and Churchill only dismissed them rather less frequently. However, if the military leaders built no popular legends around themselves, their standards of competence were very high: men like Slim, who helped win the war for Britain in Burma, Zhukov, the outstanding Russian general, or Guderian, the German genius of tank combat, were, by any standards, masters of warfare.

Some of the generals and other military leaders were more dominating, impressive and engaging figures. The British General Montgomery with his beret, the dashing commander of the German Afrika Korps, Rommel, the far-sighted Admiral Yamamoto of Japan with his great popular following, are memorable and romantic figures. At a lower level, men such as Orde Wingate, who played a brilliant and unconventional part in Britain's fighting in Ethiopia and Burma, will be remembered as outstanding characters with special skills and talents to contribute.

Admiral Isoroku Yamamoto (1884-1943)

The Second World War changed its character, methods and fields of action many times during its course. A series of decisive, surprise masterstrokes temporarily gave the advantage to one side or the other – for example, the German breakthrough on the Meuse in May

1940 which led to the fall of France, Hitler's surprise attack on the Soviet Union on 22 June 1941, or the Allied landings on the Normandy beaches on 6 June 1944. All of these were masterstrokes, but for pre-emptive brilliance (ruthless but effective) surely nothing can touch the surprise attack by the Japanese on the American battle fleet at Pearl Harbor. On the morning of 7 December 1941, in just under two hours, the fleet was knocked out at minimal cost to the Japanese. What makes this feat even more memorable is that the conception and planning of it were substantially the work of one man, certainly one of the greatest strategic geniuses of the war: the Japanese grand admiral Isoroku Yamamoto.

He was born on 4 April 1884, into a poor family (his father was a village schoolmaster), but one that was descended from the *samurai*, the ancient Japanese warrior class. Japan had already embarked on her race to rival the West and also to dominate her gigantic but weakened neighbour, China. In such a world, and with family traditions such as his, it was natural that Isoroku Yamamoto should choose a military career, and at 15 he became a cadet in the great new Western-style navy that Japan was building. As a young ensign, he fought in the great naval battle of Tsushima in 1904 which brought the Russo-Japanese war to a successful conclusion for the Japanese. In this battle he was wounded in the right leg and lost two fingers of his left hand.

In the Japanese navy of the inter-war years, he progressed rapidly, becoming a rear-admiral in the early part of the 1930s and the chief technical planner for the navy. In the 1920s he had studied as a naval attaché in the United States, at Harvard, and had become fascinated by the new dimension of air power which was transforming traditional naval warfare. It was he who insisted that the Japanese equip themselves with aircraft-carriers, at the expense of the traditional, heavy battleships which more conventional minds still preferred. He was also instrumental in the construction of torpedo planes, long-range bombers and the fast fighters to fly off the decks of the carriers, the

6 Admiral Isoroku Yamamoto, far-sighted planner of Japan's naval war.

famous Zero aircraft. In all this he showed himself a man of originality and insight, devoted to the greatness of his country as almost all Japanese were. He was also a man of humanity, although very tough when he believed his duty demanded it: he insisted on maximum night-flying training for his pilots under dangerous conditions, and this led to many deaths.

In 1939, when the war in Europe began, Japan was engaged in a loose understanding with Germany and Italy (the Axis powers), and was conducting a war to dominate China on land. Her relations with the United States, with whom she disputed mastery of the Pacific, were tense; war was being predicted by many experts on both sides. Yamamoto, who knew America at first hand, was absolutely convinced that, because of the huge economic power of the United States, Japan would have no chance of winning a prolonged war with her, and he made this view clear to other national leaders. This was a brave stand in a society gripped by war-fever where many younger officers believed it was their duty to assassinate those who were soft-hearted.

However, as tension grew, Yamamoto began to believe that war must eventually come, and he came to the conclusion that the best plan would be to make a decisive, pre-emptive strike which would weaken the United States and force her to seek an early peace. The Pacific base of the United States fleet was at Pearl Harbor in the Hawaiian islands. From early in 1940, Yamamoto began planning the blow that would knock out this fleet. He was now Naval Commander-in-Chief, but he found that his plan met with great opposition, from within the naval ministry and even from his own staff. The Japanese fleet would have to sail far into Pacific waters before the blow could be delivered, surprise was essential and most Japanese leaders thought the risk was too great.

In late 1941 President Roosevelt of the United States placed a total embargo on oil supplies to Japan and it was seen that this would lead to the strangulation of the Japanese economy. Now the Japanese were ready for war and Yamamoto's plan was accepted. It was kept very secret, and most top ministers did not know where the blow was to be struck.

The Japanese attack on the fleet stationed at Pearl Harbor, delivered with the Japanese fleet 300 miles away, began shortly before 8 a.m. on the morning of Sunday, 7 December, 1941. It was preceded by no formal declaration of war (the Japanese ambassador was supposed to deliver one half-an-hour before the attack, but he was late). During less than two hours of bombing the American Pacific fleet practically ceased to exist. The Americans lost 349 aircraft, four battleships and ten warships, while more then 3,500 American servicemen and civilians were killed or injured. By contrast, the Japanese sent in 360 aircraft of which only 29 were lost. It was a ruthless stroke, but, nevertheless, a feat of strategic genius. In Japan, Yamamoto immediately achieved the status of a national hero; in America he was built up into a treacherous monster.

The great victory at Pearl Harbor was followed by the astonishingly rapid conquest by the Japanese of almost the whole of south-east Asia, including the great British naval base of Singapore and on to the gates of British India. Yet it has been questioned how wise the attack on Pearl Harbor was. It was not a complete victory: the oil installations were not bombed, all four American aircraft carriers were away from Pearl Harbor at the time, and no attempt was made to capture the base. The attack led Germany to declare war on the United States in support of Japan, but these countries were now facing an alliance of America, the Soviet Union and Britain, the combined resources of which were so great that they must eventually win. Yamamoto himself was filled with forebodings, despite his triumph. He wrote after Pearl Harbor in letters to his sister and a fellow admiral:

Well, war has begun at last. But in spite of all the clamour that is going on, we could lose it. . . . The fact that we have had a small success at Pearl Harbor is nothing. People should think things over and realize how serious the situation is.

The British Prime Minister Churchill said, in contrast, "So we had won after all."

Despite the adulation which he was now given, Yamoto spent most of his time in the simple cabin of his flagship, *Yamamoto*, continuing to warn that the war might still be lost. The Japanese had a further success at the Battle of the Java Sea in March 1942. This

7 American ships burning during the Japanese attack on Pearl Harbor.

crushed naval resistance in the Dutch East Indies. But their advance towards Australia was halted in May at the battle of the Coral Sea, where, for the first time in history, fleets fought at a range of 160 miles: the carrier had come into its own.

Yamamoto argued again that since American resources were so much greater than Japanese, Japan should aim to inflict maximum damage in minimum time. He therefore planned the battle of Midway for June 1942, almost a repeat of Pearl Harbor, with the object of destroying the remaining American fleet and opening the way to seize Hawaii (Midway Island in about half-way between Japan and Hawaii).

Yamamoto was not destined to have a second surprise success. He hoped to lure the American fleet northwards by a preliminary attack on the Aleutian Islands, but the Americans had cracked the Japanese codes, the American commander Nimitz was warned of the plan and disregarded the decoy. The Japanese set to sea with the greatest fleet in the history of the Pacific (well over 100 vessels, with eight carriers), which should have been sufficient to sink the American carriers, but the Japanese were acting in the dark and were out of contact with each other at the crucial moments. Yamamoto himself sailed with the fleet, but when on 4 June Japanese carrier-borne aircraft attacked Midway, he had lost contact with the carrier commander, Nagumo. Nagumo's planes were back on deck re-arming when the presence of an American carrier was reported to him: he could not get them away before American bombers flew in and sank all four large Japanese carriers and 330 aircraft in less than five minutes. Some historians claim that in those five minutes the war was lost for Japan. Certainly, although she still had had her conquests, she had lost the mastery of the Pacific.

Yamamoto continued to fight, using his preferred tactic of pre-emptive action. Later in June, he ordered the occupation of the island of Guadalcanal, an island in the southern Solomons, and for five months the Japanes fought the Americans for possession in a series of bloody engagements. By February 1943, the Japanese were forced to withdraw. In April, Yamamoto decided to make a personal tour of his men in the Guadalcanal area to give them new heart. Once again the Americans managed to break the Japanese codes and discover details of his exact itinerary. He was still hated by them as the instigator of Pearl Harbor and navy secretary Knox conceived, and other American leaders agreed, "Operation Vengeance", the plan to kill Yamamoto. On the evening of 17 April, 1943 a message was flashed from Washington to fighter control at Henderson Field, Guadalcanal, with orders:

Squadron 339 P.38 must at all costs reach and destroy Yamamoto and staff. . . . President attaches extreme importance to this operation . . . (John Deane Potter, *Admiral of the Pacific*)

Soon after 7 a.m. on the morning of 18 April, 16 US Lockheed Lightnings took off towards Bougainville, where they surprised Yamamoto's aircraft. He was in one camouflaged bomber, his staff in another, with an escort of six fighters. Admiral Ugaki in the other bomber describes the fate of Yamamoto's plane:

When without warning the motors roared and the bomber plunged towards the jungle, levelling off at less than 200 feet, nobody knew what had happened. . . . Our escort fighters turned towards the attacking enemy aircraft . . . but the numerically superior enemy force broke through the Zekes [the Japanese accompanying planes]. . . .

For a few minutes I lost sight of Yamamoto's plane but finally located it far to the right. I was horrified to see it flying slowly just above the jungle with bright orange flames rapidly enveloping the wings and fuselage. About four miles away from us the bomber trailed thick black smoke, dropping lower and lower. As our bomber snapped out of its turn I scanned the jungle. The Betty [Yamamoto's plane] was no longer in sight. Black smoke boiled from the dense jungle into the air.

8 Jungle creepers grasp the rotting fuselage of the burnt-out Japanese plane in which Admiral Yamamoto was travelling when he was shot down.

Minutes later Admiral Ugaki's plane was also shot down. He and other officers were later picked out of the nearby sea, badly hurt, by Japanese patrol boats, but Yamamoto was dead. One of the American admirals who had planned his death, Halsey, heard the news at a conference the next morning. His officers whooped and applauded, but he said sourly:

What's good about it? I had hoped to lead that scoundrel up Pennsylvania Avenue in chains with the rest of you kicking him where it would do the most good.

It was a poor epitaph for this great admiral, the prophet of the age of the naval carrier, a style of warfare which was born and died with him. The Japanese knew better how to honour the dead: nearly the entire population of Tokyo turned out for his spectacular state funeral, the greatest scenes of mourning for an admiral since the British had lost Nelson at Trafalgar almost 140 years before.

Marshal Georgi Zhukov (1896-1974)

The Second World War was the greatest conflict in the history of mankind, and yet it can seem rather lacking in important consequences. Few national borders were much changed by the war (Poland is the obvious exception) and few new powers emerged (America was already great, Britain already declining). Nevertheless, the war did have one enormous consequence, and that was in deciding the overlordship of eastern Europe. Germany's bid for domination of the entire continent spectacularly failed. She became a divided country, and into her place as the master of eastern Europe stepped Soviet Russia, the Communist country, which in the inter-war period had been excluded from European affairs. Russia's great military victory was paid for with the blood of 20 million dead Russians. Many great soldiers took a part in directing this war, but one took a leading role in every battle and can justly claim (with the Soviet dictator Stalin) to be the chief architect of the military victory. This was Marshal Georgi Zhukov.

He had been born on 19 November, 1896 (by old-style Russian dating) into the poverty of the Russian countryside in the last years of the Tsarist empire. His father was a village cobbler, and the family lived in a one-room cabin which once fell down from sheer dilapidation. At the age of 12, Zhukov was apprenticed to a master-furrier in Moscow, and he practised this trade until he was drafted into the Tsar's army in 1915. He became an NCO (non-commissioned officer). In this early background, he was very typical of the men who came to take high command in the next war. When Tsarism had been overthrown and the Soviet Union set up after 1917, and after the dictator Stalin had liquidated almost all the old revolutionary élite and the high command in the 1930s, power came to these hard, uneducated men of peasant origin, many of whom had been Tsarist NCOs. The bald, heavy-set, rather darkly handsome Zhukov, with his quick threats to court-martial everyone in sight and his willingness to shoot the incompetent, was a classic example of the type, although distinguished by great military and diplomatic ability.

Zhukov joined the new Red Army in 1918 and the Communist Party shortly after. He progressed well in the Soviet army during the inter-war period, but, when the European war broke out in 1939, he was still a relative unknown, although a close associate of the powerful Marshal Timoshenko. It seemed that the dictator Stalin also had his eye on this promising soldier: the pathologically suspicious Stalin trusted no one, but he was to bring himself to trust Zhukov more than most. In 1939 Zhukov was sent as commander of the Soviet First Army Group to the fighting with Japan along the Manchurian border and here he carefully and methodically built up his forces, until in a crushing attack he destroyed the Japanese Sixth Army. The campaign established the Zhukov style of warfare: methodical, dealing in massive hammer blows rather than clever tactical strokes and not sparing of human life. It was certainly effective; during the war (until the very end), although the neighbours were part of opposing alliances, there was no fighting between Russia and Japan. The crushing lesson from Zhukov may have persuaded Japan into signing a non-aggression pact with Russia in 1941, only weeks before Germany attacked Russia in the West.

In January 1941, five months before Germany attacked, Zhukov became army Chief of Staff. The method of his appointment was typical of the capricious, frighteningly sudden way Stalin ran the country. The previous Chief of Staff was Kirill Mereckov. One day, after an important military exercise, Stalin summoned his commanders to the Kremlin and ordered Mereckov to report on the exercise. He was unprepared and flustered badly. When he finished, Stalin said, "Comrade Timoshenko has requested that Comrade Zhukov be named Chief of the General Staff. Do you all agree?" They all agreed; people usually did when Stalin spoke. As suddenly as that, Mereckov was out, Zhukov in.

Germany's surprise dawn attack on the Soviet Union came on 22 June, 1941, and initially threw the country into total confusion. Fifteen hundred aircraft were destroyed on the ground, and the Germans swept hundreds of miles into Russia, taking at least 2 million prisoners of war by October, many of whom they later murdered in camps. Zhukov now took on the role he was to have throughout the war: that of Stalin's troubleshooter who could be rushed into a crisis spot to infuse local commanders with his own savage determination or send them to the firing squad. He quickly became known as "the general who never lost a battle", and indeed he won the first victory of Russian arms over the Germans at the battle of Yelnya, 220 miles west of Moscow, in early September 1941. His fellow marshal and national hero, Konstantin Rokossovsky, sums him up in these terms:

Zhukov was always a man of strong will and decisiveness, brilliant and gifted, demanding, firm and purposeful. All these qualities, unquestionably, are necessary in a great military leader and they were inherent in Zhukov. It is true that sometimes his toughness exceeded what was permissable. . . . In the heat of the fighting around Moscow Zhukov sometimes displayed unjustified sharpness. . .

What Zhukov's "sharpness" could mean for

9 and 10 Contrasting faces of the German and Russian armies in 1943: (*above*) the smiling Russian tank crew; (*below*) the despairing German soldier, alone and wondering what to do next.

the ordinary Russian infantryman is demonstrated by a conversation he had with the American general Eisenhower, after the war. Eisenhower had been describing the elaborate methods the Americans used to clear minefields – flails, sweeps, and so on. Eisenhower reports Zhukov's answer:

If we come to a minefield, our infantry attack exactly as if it were not there. The losses we get from personnel mines we consider only equal to those we would have got from machine guns and artillery if the Germans had chosen to defend the area with strong bodies of troops instead of minefields.

There were other barbarities: the secret police (NKVD) formed "retreat-preventing formations" which shot any man who went back under fire; Russian prisoners-of-war were also deemed to have retreated and, at the end of the war, those who survived German captivity mostly went straight to Soviet labour camps.

Despite such attitudes, Zhukov seems to have been popular with the troops and certainly became a national hero. It was an infinitely hard war that was fought amid the Russian snows, totally different from that fought on the West European and African battlefields. The Germans fought a naked war of conquest and exploitation: they massacred Communists, prisoners of war and Jews. In fighting this savage enemy, and despite the cruelty with which they were often treated by their own rulers, the Russians developed an immense feeling of national purpose that was to carry their victorious armies all the way to devastated Berlin. Zhukov was associated with all the battles that marked their progress.

In December 1941, the Germans were approaching Moscow, and advance units actually reached the tram terminus on the outskirts of the capital. In October Zhukov had been called from Leningrad and appointed Commander-in-Chief of the whole Russian western front, and it was he who launched the counter-offensive on 6 December which saved Moscow from capture. He also planned the next great battle, to hold Stalingrad against the Germans at the end of 1942 and beginning of 1943, and in July 1943, he launched the Kursk offensive, the greatest tank battle of the war and the decisive victory which enabled the Russians not only to clear the Germans from their own soil but also to conquer and dominate all Eastern Europe besides.

Stalin and Zhukov developed one of the closest collaborations of the war, although it was not always an easy relationship. Once, early in the war, Stalin complained that Zhukov had not been sufficiently offensive, and made him retire as Chief of Staff and take command at the front. Zhukov was about to storm off when Stalin suddenly smiled, told him not to get upset and invited him to have a cup of tea. There were some who thought that Zhukov had developed an unhealthy ascendancy over Stalin and certainly he was one of the few who ever dared contradict the Commander-in-Chief, but Zhukov was still kept on the rein. In his memoirs he describes a military conference in December 1941 when he argued for a limited offensive, whilst his fellow commander Timoshenko had already proposed a general one to Stalin:

"I have discussed it with Timoshenko," Stalin said, "He is for the offensive. We must pound the Germans to pieces as soon as possible so they won't be able to mount an offensive in spring."

Stalin then asked, "Who else would like to speak?" There was no reply. "Well then, the discussion is over."

As we left the conference room B.M. Shaposhnikov said to me: "You shouldn't have argued, the Supreme Commander had that question settled."

"Why was my opinion asked then?"

"That, my dear fellow, I do not know," B.M. Shaposhnikov said, sighing heavily. (*The Memoirs of Marshal Zhukov*)

As the war came towards its end, and Zhukov's fame as a national leader grew, Stalin became increasingly suspicious of him. In early February 1945, Zhukov's armies were at Küstrin, only 40 miles from Berlin, and he wanted to go on and take it immediately; some say the war could have been ended then rather than in May. However, Stalin phoned and ordered him to halt. Some historians argue that this was a wise move because the army had outrun its supplies, while other say Stalin was politically motivated by a desire not to let Zhukov become too powerful. At the very end, in April, Stalin organized a race to take Berlin between the rival commanders Zhukov and Konev but it was Zhukov's forces which achieved the final honour of planting the red flag on the German parliament building, the Reichstag, and capturing Hitler's bunker. Zhukov also signed the German document of capitulation on 9 May 1945, and remained in Berlin as one of the Russian leaders at the three-power conference held at Potsdam in 1945 to settle outstanding issues of the war.

While in Berlin, the fighting over, Zhukov allowed the more genial and human side of his character to come to the fore. He describes in his memoirs how he stopped in his car once

11 The allied conquerors of Berlin near the Brandenburger Tor in July 1945: Marshal Zhukov in the centre, Field Marshal Montgomery of Great Britain on his right, Marshal Rokossovsky of the Soviet Union on the extreme right.

12 The Soviet Union honours a great soldier: guards by the Kremlin Wall where the ashes of Marshal Zhukov were laid to rest, 21 June, 1974.

and found a Russian soldier trying to take a German orphan boy home with him because his own family had all been killed. But a German woman in the crowd said the boy was her nephew and she wanted him. In his Memoirs Zhukov says:

I couldn't help intervening: "Listen, friend, when you return home you'll find yourself a son: we have so many orphans now. Still better if you take a child with its mother."

The soldiers started laughing and with them the German boy. Our soldiers gave the women and children bread, sugar, tinned meat and biscuits while the child whom our soldier held in his arms received sweets besides. The soldier kissed the boy and sighed sadly.

"What kind hearts Soviet soldiers have," I thought to myself, and going up to the soldier firmly shook his hand.

Perhaps incidents like that explain why Zhukov was liked by his troops despite their sufferings. But the great political career predicted for him by some never came about. He was soon rusticated by Stalin to a command deep in rural Russia and, although he achieved political prominence again after Stalin's death, he was again demoted. He lived in his country house with his family, wrote his memoirs and died in 1974.

Emperor Haile Selassie (1892-1975)

It has often been said that the dates usually given for the duration of the Second World War – 1939 to 1945 – apply only to a minority of the nations that took part. The meaning of this is well-illustrated with regard to Ethiopia. The emperor, Haile Selassie, supreme ruler of Ethiopia during this period, was the first victim of Axis aggression, driven from his country the the Italians in 1936, and the first to be restored by Allied arms, in 1941. Ethiopia's war had its origin not in the politics of the 1920s and 1930s, but in the country's national struggle to keep herself independent from the competing European powers that scrambled to colonize Africa in the later years of the nineteenth century. Gradually Italy marked down Ethiopia as her preferred target for colonization and the other powers accepted this. After one failed attempt in 1896, the Italians tried again in 1935-6, under their new facist dictator Mussolini, and were successful. The world stood by and did nothing. Only after Italy entered the European war in 1940 did Ethiopia's destiny become entangled with the war and the British decide to restore Haile Selassie.

This remarkable ruler was born on 23 July 1892. His father, Ras Makonnen, was governor of the provincial capital of Harar and a cousin of the Emperor Menelik who had completed the unification of Ethiopia and established his authority over the great nobles, or *rases*, of whom Ras Makonnen was one. His mother, Waizero Yeshimabeit, was probably the daughter of a former captured slave (slavery was not abolished in Ethiopia until the 1940s). From very early years, there was something regal about the small, serious young Ras Tafari (as he was generally known before he became emperor and the name by which he is known in the Rastafarian cult). His path to becoming emperor was never straightforward, and he had to fight his way to power among the ambitious *rases* and scheming court women of Ethiopian history at that period. Although a quiet, essentially peaceful man, he had been forced to become cunning; "half-man, half-snake", he was called by his enemy, the eunuch Balcha. In 1923, as Regent for the Empress Zauditu, Haile Selassie arranged for his country to join the League of Nations which he hoped would maintain the peace if Italy tried to invade Ethiopia.

In 1930 Haile Selassie became emperor; he worked hard to modernize his country, which was still in a backward state, but his plans were disturbed at the end of 1934 when Italy provoked the Walwal frontier incident (this was a well in the Ogaden desert not far from the borders of Italy's then colony in Somaliland). Italy used this incident as a pretext to launch another attempt to take over Ethiopia in 1935 and 1936. The Ethiopian armies fought bravely, but they were not equipped for modern warfare. They could not fight against the Italians under the granite-faced Marshal Graziani who bombarded them from formation planes and dropped poison gas on them.

Alone among his aggressive *rases*, Haile Selassie had never expected to win a military conflict with the Italians, although he owed it to his imperial dignity to lead a battle against them. The League of Nations, on which he had pinned his hopes, although it half-heartedly condemned the Italians' act of shameless aggression, did nothing. The governments of the Western Powers Britain and France were at that time carrying out their policy of appeasement of the dictators by which they hoped to avert war; to them the wronged Ethiopians were more an embarassment than anything else. Britain and France did impose sanctions on both sides, but these only hurt Ethiopia. When, in April 1936, the emperor was finally persuaded that he could serve his country best by going into exile, he chose Britain, and went to live with his empress Menen and children at Bath. He aroused public sympathy, but when he went to the House of Commons, the prime minister Stanley Baldwin hid behind a table to avoid being forced to acknowledge him.

Italy turned Ethiopia into a colony, and Haile Selassie went before the tribunal of the League of Nations in Geneva on 30 June 1936 to plead the justice of his cause. The journalist Leonard Mosley remembered the occasion:

Of all the memories of my youth, none remains more vividly in my mind than the appearance of H.I.M. Haile Selassie I, Emperor of Ethiopia, as he stood at the bar of the League of Nations in 1936 and pleaded with the so-called civilized governments of the world not to abandon his country. I remember him as a pathetic figure, his black cloak hung from drooping shoulder, sick from the rigours and disasters of the Italio-Ethiopian war. And yet dignity still clung to him; he looked both regal and romantic. (Leonard Mosley, *Haile Selassie*)

Despite his pleading, the world could offer little but pious horror and even that did not last long. Country after country began to recognize the Italian regime, which was building roads in Ethiopia to prove that it was civilizing the country but also shooting before firing squads all Ethiopians who had any education and could act as a focus for revolt.

In June 1940, when Mussolini entered the war to support Hitler and Britain came into conflict with Italy in North and Central Africa, Haile Selassie turned from an embarrassing deposed monarch to a potentially useful ally. In July, the Italians crossed the border from Ethiopia into Britain's colony the Sudan, and it looked as if the Sudan might be overrun. It was at this point that the British, headed by the prime minister Winston Churchill, decided to fly Haile Selassie from England to Khartoum in the Sudan to attempt to recapture Ethiopia before the Italians completely closed the Mediterranean. On 25 June 1940 his small party landed in Egypt, having to stop the night in a washroom in Alexandria ("First time I've ever had a party with an Emperor in a lavatory," commented the emperor's British

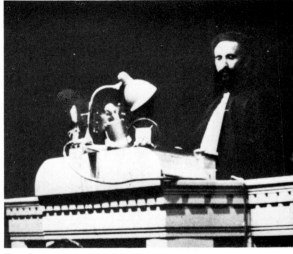

13 The Emperor Haile Selassie, dignified but alone, as he pleads the justice of Ethiopia's cause at the bar of the League of Nations.

propaganda adviser, George Steer), and then took a flying boat along the Nile. On their first night at Wadi Halfa, the emperor walked with one companion to the banks of the river, where the yellow streaks of the Blue Nile silt (from Ethiopia) were muddying the White Nile flow. The emperor took a handful from the stream, and let it run through his fingers, saying softly, *"C'est l'eau de mon pays"* ("It is the water of my country").

When the emperor arrived in Khartoum, hoping to liberate Ethiopia shortly, he found that once again the local British (or some of them) were not pleased to see him. It was only

14 Haile Selassie and Brigadier Orde Wingate plan their next move during the Ethiopian campaign of 1941.

15 Emperor Haile Selassie on the last lap of his 200-mile trek from the Ethiopian border to his liberated capital, Addis Ababa.

the favourable attitude towards Haile Selassie of the British leaders Churchill and Eden and the determination of some lower ranking officers on the spot that finally got an expedition into Ethiopia going. Foremost among these officers was an artillery officer called Orde Wingate, one of the most brilliant, unusual and controversial British leaders of the war. A brooding, self-contained man who was a deeply convinced Bible Christian, Wingate devoted himself with passion to any cause he took up; now he took up Haile Selassie and Ethiopia. He was a noted eccentric, but he usually achieved what he set out to do. He was to lead a small, irregular force called "Gideon Force" into Ethiopia and he wanted Haile Selassie to accompany it. If the emperor was to be restored, Wingate felt, it was important that he should not seem to ride in on the backs of the British: he must be in the forefront of the liberation of his country.

On 20 January 1941, soon after noon,

Emperor Haile Selassie crossed into Ethiopia with Gideon Force and raised the Ethiopian flag. The force consisted of fewer than 2000 soldiers, together with a motley collection of writers and journalists. Nevertheless, in its four months' campaign it succeeded in taking several important Italian forts. During the campaign, Haile Selassie did essential work rallying the Ethiopian tribesmen to his flag, and took part in all the hardships of the force. At the end of one exhausting march, when the emperor's face had gone green from exhaustion, Wingate kept prodding his horse to make it go faster. The emperor finally fell back saying:

You go first, Colonel Wingate. And let us hope that the people will recognise which one of us is their Emperor.

16 Ethiopian patriots applaud one of the Emperor's speeches.

At the same time as Gideon Force was marching through the highlands of Ethiopia, four other Allied armies, including British, South African, Indian, Gold Coast, Senegalese and Ethiopian troops, were converging on the Italians in Ethiopia. It was General Cunningham's largely South African force that took the capital Addis Ababa in April. The hostility to Haile Selassie of some Allied figures continued: General Cunningham sent orders that Haile Selassie was not to come to his capital to receive the homage of his people, on the pretext that, if he arrived, the Ethiopians would go wild and kill the 25,000 Italians remaining in Ethiopia. The emperor ignored this and entered Addis Ababa on 5 May with Wingate. In front of his palace, the emperor made a speech, with the fate of the Italians in mind:

On this day, which men of earth and angels of heaven could neither have foreseen nor known, I owe thanks unutterable by the mouth of man to the loving God who has enabled me to be present among you. Today is the beginning of a new era in the history of Ethiopia. . . . Since this is so, do not reward evil for evil. Do not commit any act of cruelty like those which the enemy committed against us up to the present time. Do not allow the enemy any occasion to foul the good name of Ethiopia. We shall take his weapons and make him return the way he came.

It was a great moment of triumph, although there were still problems to come. There was a large British share in the government of Ethiopia for some time, and some elements among the British even wanted to deny Ethiopia total independence and keep the country under British protection. The emperor had to fight such ideas and succeeded in winning an Anglo-Ethiopian agreement in January 1942 and in making Ethiopia a member of the United Nations, which many British had also opposed. Although the British helped Haile Selassie win back his country, they were rather ungracious allies; his continued friendship with Britain in the post-war years did him credit.

After the war, Haile Selassie continued to try to develop his country, although he did not grant it democracy. Ethiopia made strides, although there were some who through progress was too slow. Haile Selassie survived one attempt to depose him in 1960, but a second attempt in 1974 – an army coup led by Marxist officers – proved successful. The aged emperor was taken into captivity, and died on 27 August 1975, at the age of 83. The official cause of his death was given as "circulatory failure".

FIGHTERS IN THE FORCES

The armies and other forces of the Second World War, who had been conscripted largely from men doing ordinary civilian jobs, were sharply divided into two large groups: those who took part in battles and those who did not. Those soldiers who did not have to fight outnumbered those who did. The reason was that, with the increasing technical complexity and organization applied to modern war, it required a large number of men and women doing supportive work behind the lines to keep one man fighting in the front line.

This means that, for many, the war consisted of "foreign travel tempered by excessive regimentation", as the writer John Ellis put it in his book *The Sharp End of War*. A characteristic document of the war is the film *South Pacific*, where the main problem for the American soldiers at the Pacific base-camp is the shortage of "dames" (even that is soon solved by the arrival of a party of female ensigns), and the only perceptible danger is the necessity for certain soldiers to fly on "missions" to enemy-held islands. Apart from that, there is a lot of sunshine and healthy sports to play. How different such an experience was from the typical experience of the soldier in the First World War: shivering in the rat-infested trenches and facing a lonely, painful death in no-man's-land.

However, there was still a large number of men who had to face a similarly harsh experience in the Second World War. From the days of the very first wars, the central element in every army had been infantry: soldiers, fighting on foot, carrying weapons. The First World War had been almost entirely a great infantry action. Despite the application of technology to warfare and many powerful new weapons, the central importance of infantry was not lessened in the Second World War. It never became possible to win any

battle without having large numbers of men moving forward to take the next clump of bushes or enemy-held house, and facing mortars, shells, machine-guns and rockets as they did so. Warfare was faster-moving than in the first war – instead of whole battalions attempting to move a few hundred yards and being mown down by artillery fire as they did so, there was a new emphasis upon dispersal, mutual support through close radio communications, and flexible responsiveness to the local situation – but war did not change that much. There were as many trenches in the second war as in the first, and movement forward was often agonizingly slow and painful. For the fighting soldier war remained hell, as it had always been, with cold, wet and tired men, pestered by lice or flies, having to face terrifying bombardment and the ever-present possibility of dying or being disabled for life.

The newest type of land warfare in the Second World War was tank warfare, which had just started to come in at the end of the first war. During the early years of the war, tanks achieved astonishing breakthroughs in the German *Blitzkrieg* style of warfare which conquered Poland in 1939 and France in 1940. But, with the introduction of the anti-tank gun half-way through the war, and the consequent need for the infantry to go in first to clear the way, this type of warfare was slowed up and it lost much of its potential to be exhilarating. Tankmen tended to despise the foot-sloggers, although tank warfare could be just as horrifying: being slowly burned alive in a tank from which you could not escape was only the worst hazard.

Several other types of land warfare were very important. There was much more guerilla fighting than in the First World War – the Russian army was particularly keen on guerilla units and dropping parachutists behind enemy-held lines – and artillery had become immensely large and powerful, and so engineers were vital.

The Second World War was fought in all dimensions: although the majority fought on land, navies and air forces were of equal importance in many theatres. At sea, the Second World War was the great age of the aircraft-carrier, the U-boat and the destroyer.

In the air, the romantic figure of the fighter pilot held sway. The supremely skilled aircraftmen who won the "Battle of Britain" in 1940 and saved Britain from invasion or the rival aces of the German *Luftwaffe* were among the greatest popular heroes of the war; the Spitfire or Messerschmidt planes they flew remain the most popular exhibits in the military museums today.

Keith Douglas (1920-1944)

Keith Douglas was one of the finest English poets of the Second World War. He had all the sensitivity to human experience of the true poet, but this was combined with a certain hardness and detachment which made him well able to function in war. The little boy who liked playing with soldiers grew into a man who wanted, even enjoyed, the challenge of combat. To his fellow soldiers, as the writer Lawrence Durrell points out, he was not a poet, but a "brave and experienced officer of the line". The combination of soldier and poet is perhaps the chief interest Keith Douglas still has for us today.

Keith Castellain Douglas was born on 24 January 1920 into a family of the struggling middle class. Douglas got his education, largely by means of scholarships, at Christ's Hospital School and the university of Oxford, where he had finished his first year when war broke out in September 1939. In the introduction to the *Collected Poems of Keith Douglas* his tutor at Oxford, Edmund Blunden (also a poet), hints at the qualities Douglas was to bring to the war:

Keith's character was, I believe, complex in the manner of many artists. Against his generosity and zest for life must be placed, if the portrait is to be (as he would have wished it to be) true to

life, certain less endearing qualities – an impulsive and obstinate streak which was sometimes the despair of even his closest friends.

17 Keith Castellain Douglas, outstanding soldier-poet.

Keith Douglas was not called up for a year (the Second World War, in all countries, was more a matter of waiting your turn compared with the rush to enlist of the First World War), but at the end of 1940 he began training as an officer. Douglas approached his initial training, at Redford Barracks in Edinburgh, with great enthusiasm. As Desmond Graham writes in his biography of the poet:

Douglas cultivated all the simple soldierly virtues. To come to attention and salute with the vigour and precision of a Guardsman was a skill he wished to perfect. For two hours each night he "boned" his boots, softening the leather by working in a specially-made mixture, one component of which was horses' urine, and smoothing it with the back of a toothbrush. When some months later, Douglas met Raymond Pennock in Oxford he inquired whether he too boned his boots; on hearing that Pennock did not, Douglas affirmed that such things did matter. (*Keith Douglas 1920-1944*)

Douglas finally received a commission, and sailed in June 1941 in various troop ships bound for the Middle East, to join his regiment, the Nottinghamshire Sherwood Rangers Yeomanry. He remembered the last ship, which was full of around 200 women on their way to serve as nurses and office workers in the Middle East, as an "almost luxury liner".

When Douglas joined his regiment he was posted to divisional staff at the regiment's base camp behind the lines, as officer in charge of camouflage training. But there was almost no work to do, and Douglas, who saw himself as a fighting man, grew frustrated and guilty at his inactivity. A polite request to be posted to where his regiment were fighting tank battles, in Egypt's Western Desert, met with no response. Finally, Douglas's patience snapped:

The battle of Alamein began on the 23rd of October, 1942. Six days afterwards I set out in direct disobedience of orders to rejoin my regiment. My batman was delighted with this manoeuvre. "I like you, sir," he said. "You're shit or bust, you are." This praise gratified me a lot. (Keith Douglas, *Alamein to Zem Zem*)

As all the nations fighting in the Western Desert – British, Germans, Americans and Italians – knew, this battle, the second battle of El Alamein, was to be the turning-point of the North African war, and would begin the process by which Britain and her allies would gain control of the whole North African shore. No doubt, this knowledge influenced Douglas. If he were not accepted by his Colonel, he planned to drive by car to Palestine and amuse himself until he was caught and court-martialled as a deserter. But, by preference, Douglas was running away to *join* the battle.

When he made contact with his Commanding Officer, Douglas found that many of the officers in the unit had been either killed or seriously wounded in the preceding days of action, and the Colonel was so relieved at the arrival of even a single reinforcement, that the question of disciplinary action was not considered. Douglas was given charge of the two-man crew of a Crusader Tank and would go into battle the next day.

In his first day of action, Douglas, with his regiment, moved towards the fighting but did not succeed in coming close to it. This gave Douglas time to get used to the type of tank he now commanded, the Crusader Mark III, which he had never seen before. It was not until the following afternoon, that he finally engaged the enemy. His crew was firing aimlessly because of a fault in the remote control, but they surprised about 40 Germans hiding in a pit, and Douglas was able to help in taking them prisoner. That night, the whole regiment was firing at a thousand yards' range, under heavy anti-tank barrage. Douglas wrote:

I crouched in the turret, expecting at any moment the crash which would bring our disintegration. . . . These were the intensest moments of physical fear, outside of dreams, I have ever experienced. (*Alamein to Zem Zem*)

But, as the engagement went on:

18 Crusader tanks in the North African desert,
2 November, 1942.

. . . the turret was full of fumes and smoke. I
coughed and sweated; fear had given place to
exhilaration.

Darkness ended the action suddenly, and then
the regiment was pulled out of action for four
days to rest.

This pattern was to be repeated with
variations during Douglas's period of fighting
in the North African desert: sudden bursts of
action interspersed with long periods of
hanging around, with little to do but attend to
the tanks, read, exchange cigarettes, brew up
tea and fight off the myriads of flies which
covered the bodies of the men of the Eighth
Army with inflamed and painful sores.
During this period of action, at Wadi Zem
Zem in the advance on Tripoli, Douglas was
wounded and was sent back to a hospital far
beyond the lines, in Palestine, to recuperate.
There, and later waiting to return to his

regiment in Cairo, he had time to do the
writing that was to perpetuate his name, his
magnificent series of war poems and his
account of the desert fighting, *Alamein to Zem
Zem:*

. . . I never lost the certainty that the experience
of battle was something I must have. Whatever
changes in the nature of warfare, the battlefield
is the simple central stage of the war. . . . It is
exciting and amazing to see thousands of men,
very few of whom have much idea why they are
fighting, all enduring hardships, living in an
unnatural, dangerous but not wholly terrible
world, having to kill and be killed, and yet at
intervals moved by a feeling of comradeship
with the men who kill them and whom they kill,
because they are enduring and experiencing
the same things. . .

In his book, Douglas talks a lot about tank
warfare. Although conditions in a tank were
cramped and sometimes uncomfortable and
there was the constant fear of being
incinerated if the tank were hit, tank warfare

sometimes gave men a great feeling of power, which the infantry rarely experienced. Douglas wrote:

To see these tanks crossing country at speed was a thrill which seemed inexhaustible – many times it encouraged us, and we were very proud of our Crusaders; though we often had cause to curse them.

Douglas came to know what it was to kill a man, coldly and deliberately, by firing at him through the glass periscope in the turret of the tank. He dealt with this experience honestly in his chilling, impressive poem "How to Kill".

Now in my dial of glass appears
the soldier who is going to die.
He smiles, and moves about in ways
his mother knows, habits of his.

After his first few hectic days of battle, Douglas moved across the North African desert as the Eighth Army chased the Germans back across Egypt and Libya. The landscape was a strange one: the barren, totally empty wastes of desert temporarily filled with all the litter of war – burnt-out derelict tanks, smashed guns, remains of cigarette and chocolate packets and, everywhere, the dead bodies of soldiers. Douglas observed many of these bodies with the slightly cold but powerful detachment which is the characteristic note in his poetry and prose about the war:

About two hundred yards from the German derelicts [abandoned tanks], which were now furiously belching inky smoke, I looked down into the face of a man lying hunched up in a pit. His expression of agony seemed so acute and urgent, his stare so wild and despairing, that for a moment I thought him alive. He was like a cleverly posed waxwork, for his position suggested a paroxysm, an orgasm of pain. He seemed to move and writhe. But he was stiff. (*Alamein to Zem Zem*)

Also an odd mixture of understanding and detachment was Douglas's attitude to his

19 Enemy prisoners being shepherded by the British forces near El Alamein, where the decisive battle of the North African war was fought.

fellow officers (his attitude to "other ranks" seems to have varied between friendly and rather patronizing). The Sherwood Rangers were a cavalry regiment that had been transferred to tanks; but the higher officers had retained the style of an old-fashioned cavalry regiment: they were country gentlemen who approached the war with the code of honour they had learned as public schoolboys, maintaining a stiff upper-lip, speaking little and behaving in a dashing and courageous way. Rather an outsider, Douglas admired their mixture of "stupidity and chivalry": the way, for instance that the regiment's colonel, "Picadilly Jim", was eventually killed standing up in his tank to shave.

After the colonel's death, and after the ending of the war in North Africa with victory for the Allies, there was to be new work for the regiment. Shortly before Christmas 1943, they were recalled to England to begin training for the projected invasion of northern France which, it was hoped, would hasten the end of the war in Europe. Douglas landed with the rest on the Normandy beaches on 6 June 1944. Only three days later, on 9 June, he insisted on going out on a patrol with some others at the village of St Pierre. He returned to make his report when mortar fire started.

20 Supplies being unloaded on a beach in Normandy soon after the D-Day landings on 6 June, 1944. Douglas was to be killed three days after the landings.

As he was running along a ditch, a shell exploded in a tree above him, and he was killed instantly. He was 24.

Douglas had many times told friends and girlfriends that he believed he would be killed in the war. What mattered to him was that he should have taken part in the struggle, and that he should have had time to fulfil his remarkable poetic gift. This he did: of all fine English poets, though, Douglas was one of the youngest to die; even Keats lived to be 26. Before he died, in the lines he wrote about a young German soldier seen dead in the desert, Douglas also wrote his own epitaph:

For here the lover and killer are mingled
who had one body and one heart.
And death who had the soldier singled
has done the lover mortal hurt.
(from "Vergissmeinnicht")

Farley Mowat (b. 1921)

In the Second World War a special part was played by men from Britain's dominions who, without conscription in many cases, came to the aid of the mother country and fought in unfamiliar European battlefields. These men ensured that even in 1940, when all other major powers opposed to Germany had been eliminated, Britain did not fight entirely alone. Men from Canada, Australia, New Zealand and South Africa, as well as from Britain's then colonies in southern Asia and elsewhere, took part in some of the bloodiest actions in Europe, Asia and Africa. Farley Mowat, a young Canadian officer of the First Canadian Division, was one of those who survived to tell the tale and to mourn the many fellow officers and men who died in the fight for Sicily and southern Italy in 1943.

Farley Mowat was born on 11 May 1921. His father had fought, and lost an arm, in the First World War and he thus grew up with a strong military tradition. But he was a slight and essentially solitary youth, spending much of his time wandering fields and woods observing nature. Because of his build and appearance, he was known at school as "the Shrimp" and "Baby Face". However, when war came again, Farley Mowat's tradition was not to be denied. As he himself says in his account of his fighting service in the early years of the war, *And No Birds Sang:* "Peach-faced I may have been but, appearances to the contrary, I was no sickly kid."

Farley Mowat already loathed Fascism and Nazism and believed it was the duty of every able-bodied young man in freedom-espousing countries to fight against them, and so, when war was announced in September 1939 he was eager to take up arms. His first ambition, like that of so many other young men in that era, was to be a fighter pilot, but he was rejected as being too young and weighing four pounds less than the minimum requirement. Rather disgruntled, he joined his father's regiment the Hastings and Prince Edward regiment, nicknamed the "Hasty Pees", with the hope and expectation that he would see active service. As was so common in this war, there was to be a long and frustrating period of waiting before he went into the front line. Only in July 1942 was he finally posted to an overseas reinforcement draft and sailed for England. "If we get a damn good lick at the Hun, it'll be worth it," he wrote in a hastily scribbled note to his parents.

A tough period of training followed, to simulate as far as possible the conditions of actual warfare. Mowat was forced to jump unhesitatingly into a septic sewage pond while a shouting English sergeant tossed percussion grenades under him. Finally, Mowat joined First Canadian Division and was given command of Seven platoon of Able Company. This was the penal platoon, full of hard cases and misfits. Warned by Captain Alex Campbell that they were "a bunch of ruddy carnivores" whom the toughest subalterns had failed to tame, he went to face them buckling

21 Farley Mowat pictured with one of the exploration books he has written since serving as a Canadian subaltern in Italy in 1943.

22 First Canadian contingent arrives at Greenock. Those who had come to fight for the mother country were given a rousing welcome by the local population.

at the knees and made them this introductory speech:

"Listen fellows," I began meekly, "the fact is I don't really know too much about a platoon commander's job. But I'm sure as hell willing to learn. I hope you'll bear with me till I do . . . and give me a hand when I need it. Uh, liable to need it quite a lot, I guess. Uh, well, uh, I guess that's about all I've got to say."

It stunned them. They were so used to being challenged to no-holds combat by pugnacious new officers that they did not know what to do with this tail-wagging youngster with his wisp of a moustache, his falsetto tones and his plea for mercy. (*And No Birds Sang*)

Soon, it became known that the regiment was shortly to be posted abroad, and in June 1943 the unit was given four days' leave, which Mowat spent in a country hotel in some remote Scottish hills. It was a brief respite before the storm, which he was to remember as "a world beyond reality".

On the journey to the unknown destination for an assault landing, the spirits of the men on *Derbyshire*, which was part of a fast convoy sailing into the Mediterranean, were high. Farley Mowat joined in the practical joking and attended the officers' briefings. He did feel some apprehension, for death might be very near, but this was outweighed for him and his companions by excitement. As he said of them:

We were like overtrained gun dogs just released into a cloud of powder smoke, and dead keen to go.

The first months of Farley Mowat's active service were to be composed of many short, bloody actions in which, one by one, most of his fellow officers and many men were killed. This pattern began as soon as his detachment made their dawn landing from small boats on the coast of Sicily, at the heel of Italy. Mortar bombs attacked them as they landed, and Captain Campbell ordered them to take a group of buildings held by Italians near the beach. They charged forward, weapons

blasting, and were only saved from being slaughtered by a group of commandos who completed the assault from the rear of the buildings and hosed streams of lead into the buildings. Several Italians were taken prisoner in this, Farley Mowat's first action.

Having completed this engagement in the bright glare of a Sicilian morning, they began marching north, through the fierce heat and parched, empty landscape into the interior of Sicily. In one and a half days the company marched 50 miles, mainly uphill and tortured by dust and thirst. They had three hours' sleep on the journey; some men mastered the technique of sleeping on the move. On this journey they learnt that battle is only one of the hard faces of war.

The hours of marching, "standing-to" and patrolling began to be interspersed with short, sharp encounters with the enemy and battles to take towns and strategic points. Sometimes groups of enemy Germans (the Italians had mainly withdrawn with the fall of their dictator Mussolini) were encountered unexpectedly. Captain Campbell hated Germans – they had killed his father and brother in previous wars – and was determined to kill as many of them as he could. Suddenly, one dawn, 150 German infantrymen drove by in six trucks, going as reinforcements for their colleagues. Farley Mowat describes the scene:

23 Canadian troops come ashore near Reggio Calabria during the invasion of Italy, in September 1943.

A furious bellow made me turn to see Alex Campbell launching himself down the slope. He was holding a Bren tucked under his one good arm and firing quick bursts as he ran. Although a spare mag was clenched between his teeth, he was still able to roar like a maddened minotaur . . .

Alex concentrated his berserk fury on a single truck, and when he had finished firing into it from a range of a dozen yards, his consuming hatred of the enemy must surely have been sated. Within that truck twenty or more Germans writhed and died.

Sometimes Mowat himself took the lead in action:

I had my binoculars to my eyes . . . and by the sheerest fluke glimpsed a flicker of flame and a filmy wisp of smoke coming from a pile of brush on the far side of the road. . . . Mitchuk was lying next to me behind his section's Bren . . . but he could not locate the target. . . . He rolled over and pushed the butt of the gun toward me.

"You take em, Junior!" he said . . . and grinned.

The feel of the Bren filled me with the same high excitement that had been mine when as a boy . . . I had steadied my shotgun on an incoming flight of greenhead mallards. There was a steady throbbing against my shoulder as the Bren hammered out a burst. I fired burst after burst until the gun went silent. . . . Quickly Mitchuk slapped off the empty magazine and rammed a fresh one into place.

"Give 'em another!" he yelled exultantly. "You're onto the fuckers good!"

Maybe I was. It is at least indisputable that after I had emptied the second magazine there was no further firing nor any sign of life from the brush pile. On the other hand, I never actually saw a human target, so I cannot be haunted by the memory of men lying dead or dying behind their gun. And for that I am grateful.

After some time, Mowat was transferred from being a platoon commander to intelligence officer for the company: this meant that he was no longer leading men into battle, but it could still be very dangerous work. It was as intelligence officer that he left conquered Sicily and with his regiment and division began to move up the mountainous heel of Italy. Here the weather often changed from blisteringly hot to freezing cold in the mountains, while having to struggle through rain and mud added to the men's misery. Mowat just escaped being killed in a mine explosion in which seven others died, almost fell victim to shell-shock under terrible bombardment, saw the pitiful spectacle of refugees fleeing through the devastated countryside and, before the regiment had fought half-way up Italy, had to reconcile himself to the fact that vast numbers of the "Hasty Pees" who had landed in such high spirits had been killed, including his company commander and his fellow platoon commanders. He grew to hate the enemy, and yet, when he was confronted personally with Germans who were suffering the same fate as his own comrades, could not bring himself to hate individuals. He came across a dying German in a hut during an attack:

His left hand was clasping the shattered stump where his right arm had been severed just below the elbow. Dark gore was still gouting between his fingers and spreading in a black pool about his outthrust legs. Most dreadful was a great gash in his side from which protruded a glistening dark mass which must have been his liver. Above this wreckage, his eyes were large

24 Two British Tommies with their Bren guns in the mountainous wastes that were one typical landscape of the Italian campaign.

and luminous in a young man's face, pallid to the point of translucency.

"Vasser . . . please giff . . . vasser."

Reluctantly I shook my head. "Sorry, chum, I've got none. Nein vasser. Only rum, and that's no good for you."

The eyes, so vividly alive in the dying body, pleaded with me. Oh, hell, I thought, he's going anyway. What harm! I held the water bottle to his lips and he swallowed in deep, spasmodic gulps until I took it back and drank from it myself. And so . . . and so the two of us got drunk together. And in a little while he died.

Farley Mowat survived all the terrible battles in which he fought and, at the end of the war in Europe, emerged with the rank of captain. Since the war, he has become one of Canada's foremost writers of nature and exploration books.

Lev Joffe (b. 1924)

Lev Joffe saw action with one of the specialist units of the Soviet army fighting against Germany: the forces of parachutists who sometimes jumped to earth beyond the German lines. This was skilled and dangerous work, and the men had greater scope for independence and daring than ordinary Russian soldiers, who were driven on across country by their leaders and died in scores from bullets and shells.

Lev Joffe was born in 1924 into a Soviet Jewish family. He was born in the Ukraine, not far from Kiev, but grew up in Leningrad. There, he remembers, as an adolescent, going out into the streets with other boys to do mischief in the black-out during the "winter war" against Finland in 1939 and 1940. (The Soviet Union had a pact with Germany from 1939 to 1941, and only joined the war against Germany when she was attacked by the Germans.) The Soviet Union had made few preparations for arranging black-outs and at first the darkness was total: after a month it was decreed that tiny blue lights in cars would be in order.

In 1940 Joffe moved with his mother to Moscow. Here, he soon developed the interest that was to prove so important for his future. In Gorky Park in Moscow there was a parachute tower from which young people were allowed to jump, and there was also a parachute club where, from the age of 17, they could learn to jump from planes. Joffe gave his age as one year more than it actually was, received parachute instruction from a ballerina from the Stanislavski Theatre, and by June 1941 was a trained parachute instructor.

The Soviet dictator Stalin ignored the many warnings he received about a possible German attack, although Russian peasants a friend of Lev Joffe knew predicted that before the crop was harvested there would be war. On 22 June 1941, when Germany attacked the Soviet Union, Lev Joffe was at the Moscow Aircraft Engineering Institute, which was holding an "open doors day" for young people who wanted to study there and eventually become aircraft engineers. He describes the scene, and its immediate aftermath:

A group of us were standing in the corridor waiting to be admitted to one of the labs. It was between nine and ten o'clock in the morning. Suddenly we saw a girl running towards us hysterically shouting, "War! War! War!" The attack had begun at dawn, in fact, but this was the first we had heard of it. Later, Molotov [a Soviet leader] came on the radio and announced that we were at war.

25 Soviet paratroops in training.

26 Group of Soviet parachutists boarding a plane during the drills which preceded an operation.

Those first few days of war were, in a way, utter confusion. On the second day we heard of the Churchill speech on the BBC offering support to the Soviet Union, which encouraged us no end. It soon transpired that our age group was not to be called up for another year, and I could have started at the Institute in the autumn. But I wanted to fight. I had no love for the Soviet system, but I was a Jew and the Germans had come to exterminate Jews. I knew which side I had to be on.

The members of my parachute club had, almost to a man, gone to the front. But I phoned up a man I knew who used to be a champion parachutist, Colonel Pozharov, told him I wanted to fight, and asked if he could help. I only found out much later that this man was a NKVD [the Soviet Secret Police] colonel and was also training NKVD assassins. A friend of yours in the secret police and you know nothing about it; that is the horror of the Soviet system.

In spite of his more sinister responsibilities, Pozharov was able to arrange for Lev Joffe to become a sergeant in the parachute corps, training officers and men for jumping. Lev Joffe remembers:

I immediately met lots of mates from the parachute club, so adjustment to being in the army wasn't difficult.

After two months he was directed to the staff of the partisan (guerilla) movement of the Volkov front, men who croesed over in raids into German-occupied territory (there was no clearly defined front line in all areas). When Joffe arrived with his parachute, he found he had been sent to a group without an airfield or a single parachute. They were under the direct control of the NKVD, but as long as they succeeded in subverting the Germans, they were allowed to do much as they pleased. Lev Joffe remembers them as "a pampered guerilla movement living in a frontier-like atmosphere". Many of them were very young, drank a great deal of vodka and spirits, and lived with the women of the village whose husbands were fighting at the front. Lev Joffe remembers that once a guerilla coming back from a raid late at night discovered there was another man in the house with his girlfriend. He made a network of explosives around the house and blew it sky high. He was sentenced to death, but this was commuted to serving at the front with the infantry, a hard fate for one of the "pampered" guerillas.

While he was with the guerillas, Lev Joffe did not go on their raids but worked as an instructor, teaching recruits how to lay explosives and so on. But, suddenly in January 1942, he was summoned to the Alexandrovka airfield to join a detachment of trained paras who were to jump behind German lines and destroy an important bridge. He tells the story:

We all jumped down towards the bridge on the railway line in the area of Luga and Strugi

27 Soviet YAK-9 fighter plane in flight.

Krasnye in the countryside south of Leningrad. But the jump had been recklessly arranged, and a German company was guarding the bridge as we fell to earth. As my parachute opened, I was conscious of shooting from beneath. All those young men, whom I had only met the previous day, were being killed, mostly as soon as they reached the ground. A half-moon was appearing, allowing the Germans to pick them off easily.

But I and another boy landed on the other side of a very high embankment and there was a nearby forest. We ran into it, this other boy, who was called Misha and I, in order to take cover. When the shooting had stopped and the moon was gone, we crawled towards the embankment and through a concrete water-pipe that went through the embankment. Then we saw all our comrades lying there. At first we thought they were all dead, but eventually we found a wounded chap, whose leg was damaged. We bandaged his wounds as best we could. He came with us as we left that area.

They spent the next 18 days behind German lines, with a compass but no map. They did not dare trust the local people in case they gave them away to the Germans, and so they could only move around at night, sleeping rough during the day and stealing most of their food. But the wounded man was slowing down their progress.

Eventually we took the risk and went to the house of an old woman, an isolated house not in a village. "Can you help a human being?" we said to her. She agreed and gave him the clothes of her dead husband. I never found out what happened to him.

At last they found their way back to Russian-held territory but were immediately apprehended by a Russian patrol.

. . . they were very suspicious of any one who had come from behind the German lines and took us to SMERSH [the secret police]. We were interrogated by a secret policeman who shouted at us that we were spies. He hit my friend hard on the skull. Then we were locked in a cold barn for four days, although we had given the fullest details of what had happened to us. Misha and I had become good friends by this time. Eventually they believed us and we were released.

Lev Joffe seems to have been quite lucky in the way he was treated; many of those who had been into foreign country unsupervised ended up in labour camps, such was the suspicion of the Soviet authorities. Joffe made two further jumps beyond Germans lines. The last jump was at least as eventful as the first.

This was a military mission to the guerillas who were working behind German lines. Only two of us were jumping, and they mainly wanted to send a medical orderly. But there was room for two parachutists in the plane, so I was sent too, without precise instruction. We flew in the night, and were looking for two bonfires on the edge of a lake which would have been lit by the guerillas as a signal. The pilot, Nechayev, saw two dots on the ground which he thought were the bonfires. But I don't think they can have been: but the medical orderly had jumped, so I had to jump too. I discovered to my horror that I was jumping down right towards a village, lit and full of people, and I could hear the concertina playing. . . . As I landed, I saw some people running towards me. I pulled out the stopper [of his hand-grenade] as I landed and they fell on the ground. Then, one of them said, "*Doctor*, don't throw your hand grenade." That made me realise that these must be the guerillas I had come to contact, because they were expecting the medical orderly. They thought I was him.

So I had to get rid of the grenade. As soon as I threw it, it would explode in four seconds. So I was crawling in the muddy snow with the grenade. Finally, I managed to throw it into a ditch and take cover as it exploded.

Lev Joffe was reunited with "the doctor" and remained with the guerillas behind the German lines for ten months until the spring of 1943. There was little fighting during this time – the guerillas were mainly attempting to blow up railway lines, and once got one with a train on it – as they preferred to retreat when they saw any largish German force approaching. Their main work was in harassing the peasants in the villages. The peasants remembered that they had been forced into collective farms by the Soviet authorities in the 1930s, an operation in which millions had died in deliberately engineered famines, and they were often at least as sympathetic to the German invaders as to their Soviet masters. The Germans could not garrison every village, but often left them under the control of a German-appointed Russian "elder", often an old man. Sometimes, when the Germans were far away, the Soviet guerillas would swagger into a village and shoot the elder. Often the village

28 A group of Soviet partisans prepare an explosion on a railway line in the Crimea in 1943.

people would beg for the elder's life and in those cases he might be left with a warning that if he did collaborate with the Germans again he would be shot.

In 1943, Stalin issued the "guerilla order" by which those people serving with guerilla formations who had been wounded could be discharged from the army. Lev Joffe had received a wound to his right leg, and took advantage of this opportunity to return to his earlier intention of studying aircraft engineering. He went to back to the institute in Moscow, a city he remembers at that time as "cold, dirty and unpleasant to live in". But the Ministry of Aircraft Engineering soon found out that he was a trained parachutist, and told him he was needed as a parachute tester. He could not argue.

So he went to one of the aircraft factories where the YAK 9 fighters were then being produced. He tested the parachutes of all the fighter pilots before they flew, repacking the parachute after every jump and renewing it after every 30.

Lev Joffe was still doing this work when the war ended in 1945. He then returned to his aircraft engineering studies but spent five years in a labour camp during the last tyrannical years of Stalin. He later became journalist dealing with industrial and engineering topics. In the 1960s, he defected to the West, where he has continued with his journalistic career and still enjoys parachute-jumping.

FIGHTERS ON OTHER FRONTS

Wars are not won only by military men, particularly not modern wars. In the Second World War an immensely active and sometimes dangerous role was played by those who were not members of the armed forces, or who were in the armed forces but had other fields of action. These people had very varied roles: spies, resisters, doctors and nurses, stretcher-bearers, entertainers and war artists. But all contributed in some way to their country's struggle.

The most numerous of these people were civilian resisters to military forces, and in the European context this meant resistance to Nazism. From 1940 to 1944 Hitler's Germany had under her control the greater part of Europe; although organized military resistance was not possible during this period, everywhere the swastika flag flew there were people prepared to do what they could to resist. The Nazi rulers intended to exploit Europe, and German soldiers carried out their plans; initially, people in the conquered countries did not know how to respond to the Germans, but they made themselves hated, even in western Europe where their rule was relatively mild; in eastern Europe, where they massacred and enslaved civilians, the hatred was much greater. Resistance could take all sorts of forms: information collection, sabotage, running escape lines, publishing illegal newspapers, strikes and go-slows, guerilla movements. Even a group of people falling silent in a shop when a German soldier entered were resisting. Perhaps resistance could be most effective when resisters could receive arms and pass information to agents of the Allied powers: the SOE (Special Operations Executive) was the most important British organization specializing in such work, and the story of Noor Inayat Khan, one of its agents, is told here. Resistance alone could not get rid of the Nazis, but its work was important, not least in preserving the national pride of the conquered peoples and helping them build for the future.

In Germany itself, there was little resistance. This is understandable: resistance was directed against a conquering power, but a German who resisted his own government would be branded a traitor, and would be fighting his own people and the police state. There was a widespread conspiracy to get rid of Hitler and the Nazi regime, and its members were often exceptionally brave and good-hearted, but they were more plotters than resisters on the European pattern. Among the civilian population not connected with the plot, there was only one outstanding example of resistance – the group of Munich university students, known as the "White Rose," consisting of Hans and Sophie Scholl, Alexander Schmorrell, Christoph Probst and their friends, who distributed leaflets attacking the evil regime – and they were all executed. These noble young men and women did something to save the honour of Germany.

A particularly dangerous form of resistance in Nazi-dominated Europe was to help Jews who were trying to escape from extermination by the Nazis: such people usually faced execution themselves if they were caught. There were many such "righteous gentiles" in Europe, and it is perhaps unfair to single out one as being more outstanding than all the rest. But if there is one, then it is Raoul Wallenberg, the Swedish diplomat, whose story is told here and who, with single-minded courage, saved the lives of many thousands of his fellow human beings.

The Second World War swarmed with spies and agents: Stalin's "Lucy" ring in

Switzerland, his particularly successful agent in Tokyo Richard Sorge, the double-agent Mathilde Carré ("the Cat") and many others. There were some outstanding intelligence triumphs in the war, such as the comprehensive breaking of German cipher organization achieved by the British ULTRA codebreaking organization. But agents could also rebound heavily against their employers: the British used their success to "turn around" every single German agent working in Britain.

Scientists played an important role in the war, often developing new weapons to carry on the fight: the German Wernher von Braun who developed the V2 rockets or the men such as Fremi and Oppenheimer who worked on the atom bomb are well-known examples. Among many exceptional doctors and nurses of the war, a special place of honour is held by Archibald McIndoe, the New Zealand surgeon working in Britain, who did so much to help the badly burned. The agony of the burned fighter pilot ("one moment has turned him from a Don Juan into an object of pity, and it's too much for him to bear") aroused all his powerful compassion, and the fliers who came under his care owed an enormous amount of reborn hope to him.

Artists and entertainers interpreted the struggle for ordinary people and helped to give meaning to their fight. Britain was particularly rich in distinguished war artists: Graham Sutherland, Paul Nash, John Piper, Laura Knight, Edward Ardizzone. The men and women who sang and entertained the troops – in England, names such as Vera Lynn, Gracie Fields, Beatrice Lillie, Cicely Courtneidge, Tommy Handley – were held in special affection for the spirit and generosity with which they used their gifts, and songs such as "Lili Marleen" or "We'll Meet Again" are more poignant than anything else for those who lived through the war.

Fabian von Schlabrendorff (1907-1980)

Fabian von Schlabrendorff was one of the most determined and daring of the Germans who resisted Hitler and who tried to depose or kill him. What also makes him remarkable is that he survived the war while almost all the others implicated in the bomb plot of 20 July 1944 against Hitler, or more loosely implicated in the resistance, went to the gallows or faced a firing squad. He owed his escape to an amazing series of coincidences and thus lived to bear witness to the dedication of the thousands who did not share his luck.

Von Schlabrendorff was born in 1907 into a family of the Brandenburg nobility, and

29 Fabian von Schlabrendorff in London in 1966 to promote his book *The Secret War Against Hitler*. The following year he became a German constitutional judge.

qualified as a lawyer. Bespectacled and intellectual-looking, silent and mild in his manners, Schlabrendorff was far from most people's idea of a conspirator and man of action. But he was a determined anti-Nazi from the start, an inveterate plotter with a marked taste for direct action. He became noted as a lawyer who would take on cases which might bring him into conflict with the Nazis and which other lawyers would not touch.

When war broke out von Schlabrendorff was busy trying to collect support for a resistance movment against Hitler and building up links with foreign statesmen who might provide support. On the very day war was declared, 3 September 1939, he was having lunch with the Counsellor at the British Embassy, Sir George Ogilvie-Forbes, in Berlin's exclusive Hotel Adlon. Von Schlabrendorff describes the scene:

While we were talking, several SS officers appeared at the door. They spoke to the head waiter and then came towards our table. I feared that they had come to arrest me, lunching as I was with an English diplomat after the outbreak of war between England and Germany. Fortunately they paid no attention to me and left again after a short conversation with Sir George. The latter had not for a moment lost his composure, and told me to my relief that the SS officers had merely given him some details of the arrangements for the imminent departure of the staff of the British Embassy. (Von Schlabrendorff, *Revolt against Hitler*)

In October 1939 Schlabrendorff was called up into the army as a non-commissioned officer. He served initially with an infantry regiment on the defensive Siegfried Line, near the French-German border. But, at the beginning of 1941, Major General Henning von Tresckow, chief of staff to Army Group Centre on the eastern front and an old friend of Schlabrendorff's, had him transferred to serve as his staff officer and as a lieutenant. Thus began an exceptionally close association.

Von Tresckow, an aristocrat like many of the conspirators, was outstanding among the leading army figures who hoped to inspire an armed revolt against Hitler. He was a brilliant soldier and a man of great sensitivity, with a rare gift for inspiring others. Tresckow had called Schlabrendorff to him as a political adviser to act as his right-hand man in organizing resistance. In any plot to overthrow the Nazi regime the assassination of Hitler was necessary to remove the co-ordinating force at the head of the Government and to release the soldiers from their solemn oath of loyalty sworn directly to Hitler as their leader. A succession of young men offered themselves as Hitler's killer, often being prepared to sacrifice their own lives, if necessary. Among these men, not surprisingly, was von Schlabrendorff acting in close collabroation with von Tresckow.

Early in March 1943, Hitler announced his intention of leaving his East Prussian headquarters and visiting Army Group Centre which was then in Smolensk in European Russia. Here was an ideal, and rare, opportunity to strike the decisive blow. It was decided to smuggle a delayed-action bomb into the aeroplane in which Hitler would be flying back to his headquarters. German explosives had a fuse which made a low, hissing noise which might lead to discovery before the bomb could detonate. But, through a military comrade, Schlabrendorff was able

30 General Major Henning von Tresckow, one of the leading army figures who plotted against Hitler.

to obtain British explosives which were silent and of which a very small amount could destroy the whole aeroplane.

Hitler appeared in Smolensk on the appointed day with his usual large escort, including his doctor and his cook, and there was a conference followed by lunch. During lunch, von Tresckow approached Colonel Brandt, one of Hitler's staff officers, and asked him whether he would take back to Hitler's headquarters two bottles of brandy for a friend there, General Helmut Stieff. The officer agreed, little knowing that the bomb was to be placed in one of the bottles with the detonator in the neck. Von Schlabrendorff and von Tresckow accompanied Hitler's party to the airport, and when he saw Hitler boarding the plane, Schlabrendorff started the fuse of the bomb: it was due to explode in half-an-hour. He handed the parcel containing the bottles to Colonel Brandt ("It required some self-control to remain calm at that moment"), Brandt stepped into the plane, it took off, and the two assassins returned to their headquarters.

However, Hitler, as was often observed, had the devil's own luck. The detonator cap failed to react, and Hitler and the brandy bottles arrived in East Prussia without anyone knowing anything was wrong. When the conspirators in Smolensk heard the devastating news that Hitler's plane had landed safely, they had another more immediate anxiety: when the brandy bottle was opened, would their plot by discovered? After considerable thought, von Tresckow telephoned Colonel Brandt to ascertain whether the parcel had yet been delivered to Stieff (who was not in the plot), because there had been some mistake. It had not, and von Schlabrendorff was dispatched the next day to the East Prussian headquarters to retrieve the parcel and substitute another. Von Schlabrendorff recalls Brandt giving it to him and then giving his hand a jerk, which made him fear a sudden detonation of the still unexploded bomb.

The attempts on Hitler's life by determined Germans did not cease, and it was the last attempt, the bomb attack by Colonel Claus von Stauffenberg on 20 July 1944, which set off the doomed attempt by the conspirators to seize control of the state. Hitler was wounded, not killed, and quick military action in Berlin foiled the conspirators' attempt. Stauffenberg and three others were shot that night, but over the next weeks and months literally thousands of people who were believed to be resisters were rounded up.

Von Schlabrendorff and von Tresckow were in Russia at the time of the attempted uprising; von Tresckow shot himself the day after the conspiracy failed and von Schlabrendorff knew that, with all the arrests, he could hardly hope to escape eventual detection. He was not surprised when he was awakened from sleep on 17 August with the announcement that he was under arrest. His first thought was to seize a pistol and put an end to his life, but he did not do so because, he says, he experienced a sudden conviction that he would eventually emerge safely from his troubles. This conviction never left him entirely through months of imprisonment and torture, and was the reason he did not try to escape, although he had more than one opportunity to do so.

31 The man von Schlabrendorff tried to kill and the dominating figure of the Second World War – Adolf Hitler (centre) at his secret headquarters along the Russian front. With him are (left) Field Marshal Mannerheim of Finland and (right) Field Marshal Keitel, chief of the German army.

He was incarcerated in the headquarters of the Gestapo, which were equipped with torture chambers, in Prinz-Albrecht Strasse in Berlin. He was in solitary confinement, but most of the other resisters were also in the prison and he caught glimpses of them:

In the past, while we had been free, it had been very difficult for these men to get in touch with each other. Now we were all together, as it were, like the cast of a bad comic opera. It is true that we were not permitted to talk; but a look, or a quickly spoken word, was often enough to secure an understanding. (*Revolt against Hitler*)

Von Schlabrendorff was tortured by the Gestapo to make him reveal information about other conspirators: spikes were driven into his fingers with a screw, his body was stretched in a form of the rack, and he was beaten to the floor with clubs many times. On one occasion he lost consciousness and the next day suffered a severe heart attack. He was tortured again, but after he admitted that his friend von Tresckow (who could not be killed because he was dead) had planned to bring pressure on Hitler to make him resign, the Gestapo left him alone for a while. He had revealed no names under torture but, as the weeks passed, he was forced to see many of his friends go from the prison to their trial under Roland Freisler of the People's Court, the Nazi regime's half-mad hanging judge. Normally, a trial before him was swiftly followed by execution.

Von Schlabrendorff appeared before Freisler with five others accused on 21 December 1944, but he was to be dealt with last, and the court did not have time that day to try and sentence him. His trial was postponed until 3 February 1945.

In these closing stages of the war, the capital of the Reich was subject to very heavy bombing by day and night and just before von Schlabrendorff's trial was due to begin (he was waiting to be called into court), the air-raid siren sounded and news came that great streams of bombers were heading for Berlin. The whole court, including the prisoner, hurriedly adjourned to the cellars. During the

32 The infamous Nazi hanging judge, Roland Freisler (centre), confronting the conspirators in the People's Court.

air-raid, the People's Court received a direct hit and a heavy beam crashed down on the head of Roland Freisler, who was still holding the files of von Schlabrendorff's case. Freisler was killed outright.

Von Schlabrendorff's trial finally took place on 16 March, with von Schlabrendorff acting as his own defence lawyer. Rather surprisingly, the court acquitted him but, as he was leaving the courtroom, the Gestapo re-arrested him. Several days later they informed him that the Court's decision had been in error but that now, as a special concession, he wound be shot instead of being hanged. Several days later he was taken to Flössenburg concentration camp in upper Franconia, which was one of the so-called "destruction camps" where anti-Nazis who had either not been tried or had been acquitted by courts were executed in batches: up to 50 people were being killed each day. Each day von Schlabrendorff expected to die, although he knew that the end of the war could now be only weeks away.

On 12 April the American army could be heard approaching the camp. All the prisoners who had not already been murdered were transferred to Dachau concentration camp. During the transfer, von Schlabrendorff's papers were lost and, when asked who he was, he lied and said he was a "prisoner of honour", a category not subjected to the usual harsh treatment. While most of the other conspirators remaining had been executed, von Schlabrendorff found himself in a barracks with a motley collection of people, ranging from a Roman Catholic bishop to a circus clown.

A few days later they were moved on to Innsbruck in Austria, and then, as the American armies relentlessly moved on, into the Puster valley near the Brenner Pass. The SS guards now began to debate what should be done with the remaining prisoners. It was decided to shoot them all at once but, before this order could be confirmed, on 4 May 1945, the company of prisoners, including von Schlabrendorff, was liberated by American troops.

Noor Inayat Khan (1914-44)

Women played an important part in the Second World War, and the conflict was one of the important stages in women's long struggle to win equality with men. Women made a special contribution in one field where they could show at least equal daring with men: resistance and espionage. The Special Operations Executive (SOE), the main British organization sending agents behind enemy lines, was prepared to use women on the same basis as men and exposed them to the same risks: of 39 women agents sent into occupied France, 13 did not return. Of these brave women who gave their lives, among the most outstanding was Noor Inayat Khan, posthumously awarded the George Cross.

SOE agents had to be able to speak fluently the language of the country to which they were sent. A fair number of them had in fact been born foreign nationals, but Noor Inayat's background was more unusual and diverse than most. She was half-Indian, half-American and had grown up largely in France. Her father was the leader of the world Sufi movement, an Indian mystical religion, and a descendant of the last Muslim ruler of southern India. Her mother was a cousin of Mary Baker Eddy, the American founder of Christian Science. Her parents went to Russia to spread Sufism there, and Noor Inayat was born in the Kremlin, the great palace of Moscow, on 1 January 1914. The family moved to England and then to France, to a suburb of Paris. There Noor Inayat grew up as a sensitive and creative child, imbued with the ideals of the Sufi movement which she helped to lead after her father's death. She studied music and medicine, and as a young woman she became well-known for her children's stories, which she published in the Sunday *Figaro* and read on *Radio Paris*. Shortly before

33 The striking looks of Noor Inayat Khan, ill-fated SOE agent in occupied France.

the outbreak of war she published a book of traditional Indian stories, *Twenty Jataka Tales*.

Basil Mitchell, later Dean of Keble College, Oxford, met Noor Inayat through the Sufi movement before the war, and talks about the personal qualities she was to bring to the unfamiliar world of the secret agent:

The lasting impression that remains with me of Noor-un-Nisa is of a very gentle creature. Her determination and practical capacity were a matter for constant surprise. Perhaps someone who knew her better, or whose insight was deeper, might have guessed at her future career, but to me this was the culminating surprise. The surprise was not her fortitude, which could have been predicted, but her capacity to sustain an active role of tough, inventive and deliberate daring. (Jean Overton Fuller, *Madeleine*)

In 1939, when war broke out, Noor Inayat trained as a nurse with the French Red Cross, thinking this would help her contribute to the struggle. In 1940, when France was about to fall to German invasion, she and her brother Vilayat decided to go to England to carry on the Sufi movement there. Accompanied by their mother and sister Claire, they left France in one of the last boats leaving the country before it capitulated. They were able to get a place because of the girls' connections with the Red Cross.

Once in England, Noor Inayat felt that to be a nurse was too trivial a contribution to make to the war, and so she joined one of the women's services, the WAAF (Women's Auxiliary Air Force) in November 1940, and trained as a wireless operator. In order to fit in, she gave her first name as Nora and her religion as Church of England.

One day, she received a letter asking her to attend for an interview at the War Office with a certain Captain Selwyn Jepson. He was the chief selector for the French section of SOE, the organization carrying out and inspiring sabotage of the German war machine in occupied territories. Her fluency in French had brought her to the attention of SOE, although she spoke both French and English with a slight accent. Once she heard of the dangerous work of an agent she accepted immediately. Captain Jepson remembers:

I see her very clearly as she was that first afternoon, sitting in front of me in that dingy little room, in a hard kitchen chair at the other side of a bare wooden table. Indeed, of them all – and they were many – who did not return, I find myself constantly remembering her with a curious and very personal vividness which outshines the rest . . . the small, still features, the dark, quiet eyes, the soft voice and the fine spirit glowing in her. (*Madeleine*)

As a cover, Noor Inayat joined FANY (Services First Aid Nursing Yeomanry), in which she became an officer: her code name in SOE was "Madeleine" and her colleagues knew her as Nora Baker. The French section of SOE had urgent need of a fully trained wireless operator to be sent to France almost immediately, and Noor Inayat was chosen even before she had finished her SOE training (she had not done security or parachute training) and even though some of her instructors reported that they thought her too gentle and dreamy to make an effective agent in the field. Colonel Maurice Buckmaster, the head of SOE French section, decided to override these factors. It is difficult to know if he did well. Noor Inayat had been brought up in a very religious and idealistic atmosphere; she had great moral strength, but little understanding of evil; although brave, she could be too trusting and indiscreet to make a perfect agent.

On 16 June 1943 "Madeleine" was landed by Lysander aircraft in France, in a country spot near Le Mans, and made her way with another agent to Paris. It took her a day to reach her contact, and during this time she did not eat because, although she had been provided with French ration books, she did not know how to use them and feared giving herself away.

After arriving in Paris she was taken to the Agricultural School at Grignon, which was the working headquarters of a large network of spies and resisters called "Prosper". It was Noor Inayat's misfortune that when she arrived in France this network had already been given away by a traitor to the German Secret Police, the *Gestapo*, and shortly after her arrival mass arrests began. Estimates of those arrested in Paris and the provinces vary between 500 and 1500. The upshot was that Noor Inayat became the only radio operator left providing contact between Paris and London. It was feared that the Germans must know of her existence also, and London headquarters offered her the chance to return to England. She refused, although she knew she was in danger, because she did not want to leave her comrades in France without communications.

During the period of the arrests she seems to have narrowly escaped being caught several times, but, when things had quietened down, she went on with her wireless transmission. She was perhaps not as discreet as she ought to have been. She was supposed to transmit only from lonely country lanes, but once she transmitted from the village where she had grown up, although this meant trusting everyone in the village not to give her away. On another occasion, having need to pass on urgent information to London, she took the risk of transmitting from the flat where she was living, a smart block facing the Bois de Boulogne where, by chance, several SS officers were also living. She was trying to fix the aerial in a tree outside her window, when a German officer came out of his flat and offered to help her fix it. He was very polite, although all radio transmission, even for private purposes, was forbidden.

This seems a little suspicious, and the question arises: did the Germans know of her existence the whole time and were they merely playing with her, allowing her to remain free and transmit? They certainly had her code name and her general description, and later a Gestapo official was to boast that he had literally watched her arriving in France from the shadows. It is difficult to know how much they knew, but what is certain is that after about three months in France Noor Inayat was betrayed to a Gestapo agent. She was taken to Gestapo headquarters in Paris, 84 Avenue Foch. Her captor, SS Sturmbannführer Kieffer, remembers the defiance she adopted from the start:

She glared at me as if she were a caged tiger, but she wouldn't speak. (M.R.D. Foot, *SOE 1940-6*)

Within half-an-hour of her arrival at Avenue Foch, she demanded a bath, and used the opportunity to try to escape over the roof.

34 The roads of war — French refugees flee the Germans in 1940.

35 The taking of the oath at Les Invalides, Paris, by members of the Milice — the French equivalent of the German Gestapo — while Gestapo chiefs look on.

During her weeks of formal interrogation she said nothing, but she was eventually tricked into confiding in a plain clothes interpreter who told her that he was Swiss. She had also kept a record, in a school exercise book, of all the messages she had exchanged with London, in both code and clear. She had been warned repeatedly not to do this, but a wireless operation handbook she had been given said, "you must be extremely careful with the filing of your messages". This merely meant that she should keep a record of their numbers, but she became confused; perhaps the fact that she had not received full training accounts for her mistake.

The Germans had little difficulty in cracking her code and continued to work her station, sending misleading messages to London. When SOE landed three agents on the plain west of Chartres at a rendezvous arranged through her station, the Gestapo were waiting to take them into immediate captivity.

The rest of Noor Inayat's story can be briefly told. After a second unsuccessful attempt to escape from Avenue Foch, she was classed as a dangerous and uncooperative prisoner. She refused to give an undertaking that she would not escape again and so was sent to prison at Pforzheim in Germany. During the first weeks of her imprisonment she was kept all day with chains round her hand and feet. These were taken off only so that she could eat. Later, the regime relaxed a little and she spent some of the rest of her ten months' imprisonment writing more of the children's stories for which she had shown such a talent.

On 6 July 1944 she and three other women agents were taken to Dachau concentration camp, travelling in the reserved compartment of an express train. They had bread, sausages and English cigarettes, and talked animatedly during the journey. They arrived at Dachau at midnight and were shot dead, it is thought immediately upon their arrival.

Raoul Wallenberg (b. 1912)

One of the most remarkable of the stories of courage and humanity of the Second World War is that of Raoul Wallenberg. At great personal risk to himself, this young Swedish diplomat went around Hungary rescuing Jews who were due to be transported to the camps to be exterminated. It is thought that this one man may have been responsible, directly or indirectly, for saving the lives of up to 100,000 Jews. What makes the story of Raoul Wallenberg so remarkable and terrible is that, after having fought so bravely against one of the worst tyrannies of the century, he immediately fell victim to another that matched it for horror. Instead of enjoying the world's gratitude, he has lived out his days in Soviet captivity.

Raoul Gustav Wallenberg was born on 4 August 1912. The Wallenbergs were one of the most famous and distinguished families in Sweden: family members included bankers, diplomats and bishops of the Lutheran Church. Wallenberg grew up as part of a devoted, indeed unusually close family and, as his half-sister Nina put it, Raoul "gave and received so much love that he grew up to be an unusually generous, loving and compassionate person". Despite his distinguished background, Wallenberg had initial difficulty in finding a career: at the age

delight in an atmosphere of joy and youth, without a fear for the future.

We had a marvellous lunch, and then we lay in the grass, among the flowers, and talked and talked, and laughed a lot. I can't remember what we talked about. All I can remember is that sense of bliss at the release from winter, and of delight in each other's company. (John Bierman, *Righteous Gentile*)

On the last day of that May, he proposed marriage to her, but she was uncertain, telling him she was very young (she was 18 to his 31). Some time later, he telephoned her to say he was going to Budapest on a mission for the Government, that might prove dangerous: she was never to see him again.

The mission on which Wallenberg had been sent was to save as many of the Hungarian Jews as possible from extermination by the Nazis, by any means possible, but largely through the issuing of Swedish passports and taking Jews under protection of the Swedish crown. Why Budapest? Because here was the only substantial Jewish community left in Europe which Nazi persecution had not yet touched. In March 1944 there was a German occupation of Hungary and the deportation of Jews to concentration camps began. By the time Wallenberg arrived, in July 1944, there were just 200,000 terrified Jews left, cooped up in the capital.

The sending of a Swedish emissary had been organized by the Swedish Foreign Office in co-operation with the War Refugee Board, set up by President Roosevelt of America and the International Red Cross. Wallenberg must have seemed in many ways an unconventional choice for the mission. One factor may have influenced it beside Wallenberg's capabilities, his compassion and his famous name: he was himself one-sixteenth Jewish, adding just that measure of extra identification and understanding to help this sorely harassed people.

Even before Wallenberg's arrival in Budapest, the Swedish legation had started to issue protective passes (*Schutzpässe*) to

of thirty-one, while the war was on but Sweden remained neutral, he was working as a junior partner in an importing and exporting firm, the Central European Trading Company, run by a refugee Jew called Koloman Lauer. Wallenberg lived a comfortable bachelor life in Stockholm, but he suffered inner frustration and disappointment: surely this mundane work was not all that he was to do with his life.

Jeanette von Heidenstam, Wallenberg's girlfriend in the spring of 1944, later a well-known Swedish television personality, remembers the life that Raoul Wallenberg forsook, entirely voluntarily, to go on his dangerous mission. She, Wallenberg, and another couple had an open-air lunch in Stockholm's Djurgörden Park on 1 May 1944:

It was a joyful day, everything just perfect – or so it seems to me looking back – a day of pure

37 Jews besiege the Swedish legation in Budapest hoping to receive Swedish protective passports.

Budapest Jews, but it was uncertain how much notice Eichmann, the chief organizer of the extermination of the Jews, and his henchmen would take of these. Wallenberg's first task when he arrived was to design a new document to issue to the Jews, an impressive yellow and blue document embellished with the triple crown which was the official insignia of the Swedish Government: it looked like a real Swedish passport and could be used to overawe ignorant Nazi bullies. Wallenberg was only allowed by the Hungarian Foreign Ministry to issue 2500 of these passports, but eventually he issued three times that number, bribing and blackmailing Hungarian officials to turn a blind eye. He also organized hospitals, nurseries and soup kitchens for the Jews, as well as Swedish-protected houses for them to live in.

38 Jewish women being marched through Budapest on their way to forced labour. (Photograph by Raoul Wallenberg)

Despite the Nazi occupation, the Hungarian regent, Horthy, still had some limited authority in Hungary; he knew that Germany's final defeat could not be long delayed, and he exerted himself to save the remaining Jews from deportation. He succeeded in getting Eichmann and his subordinates recalled to Berlin. Persecutions of Jews continued, but for a while they were not being deported. However, when the Germans got wind of a plan by Horthy to negotiate a separate peace for Hungary with Russia, Horthy was deported to Germany, and a new government was set up in Budapest which was entirely under German control. The inevitable Eichmann returned in triumph and announced that the remaining Jews would be deported to camps in Germany.

They were moved under terrible conditions, marching up to 30 miles a day in rain and snow, driven along by the whips and rifle butts of soldiers. Many died on the way. Wallenberg with some of his colleagues started to descend on these convoys, demanding that Jews with Swedish passports should be immediately released, and also succeeding in getting others out by bluff.

Tommy Lapid, later head of the Israeli Broadcasting Authority in Jerusalem, and in 1944 living in a Swedish-protected house in Budapest, tells of his mother's experience:

One morning, a group of the Hungarian Fascists came into the house, and said all the able-bodied women must go with them. . . . My mother kissed me and I cried and she cried. We knew we were parting forever. . . . Then, two or three hours later, to my amazement, my mother returned with the other women. . . . She said one word: "Wallenberg".

I knew who she meant because Wallenberg was a legend among the Jews. In the complete and total hell in which we lived, there was a saviour-angel somewhere, moving around. . . . My mother told me that they were being taken to the river when a car arrived and out stepped Wallenberg. . . . He went up to the Arrow Cross leader and protested that the women were under protection. They argued with him, but he must have had . . . some great personal authority. He stood out there in the street, probably feeling the loneliest man in the world, trying to pretend there was something behind him. They could have shot him there and then in the street . . . instead they relented and let the women go. (*Righteous Gentile*)

Indeed, Wallenberg was risking his life constantly in his humanitarian work. True, he was a Swedish diplomat, but this would not necessarily have saved him from arbitrary murder in the disordered conditions of Budapest and, in fact, the Germans were responsible for at least one attempt on Wallenberg's life. His effrontery in the face of officials, policemen and SS knew no bounds. Once, for instance, he drove to the Budapest railway station where a trainload of Jews was about to leave for Auschwitz. The young SS officer surpervising the transport ordered Wallenberg off the platform, but Wallenberg brushed past him. His driver Sandor Ardai tells the story:

Then he climbed up on to the roof of the train and began handing in protective passports through the doors which were not yet sealed. . . . The Arrow Cross [local Hungarian fascists] began shooting and shouting at him to go away. He ignored them and calmly continued handing out passports to the hands that were reaching out for them. . . . After Wallenberg had handed over the last of the passports he ordered all those who had one to leave the train and walk to a caravan of cars parked nearby. . . . He saved dozens off that train, and the Germans and Arrow Cross were so dumbfounded they let him get away with it! (*Righteous Gentile*)

In the second week of January 1945 Wallenberg carried out his biggest life-saving coup. His private intelligence system brought him word that Eichmann's plan for the total massacre of the Jews in the Budapest General Ghetto was to go ahead. Wallenberg sent an emissary to the overall commander of the SS troops in the city, August Schmidthuber, threatening to have him hung as a war criminal if the massacre went ahead. The general hesitated, then countermanded the order.

39 Marshal of the Soviet Union F.I. Tolbouhin greets Bulgarian allies in a Hungarian town they have liberated from the Nazis.

When the Russians occupied Budapest between February and March 1945, there were 120,000 Jews left alive in the city, the only substantial Jewish community to survive in the whole of occupied Europe. They owed their lives to various factors, but it seems fair to say that the great majority would have been dead but for the efforts of Raoul Wallenberg and his helpers.

Wallenberg had made a detailed economic and social plan for the post-war relief of the Jews, many of whom were in a desperate condition because of the sufferings they had undergone. On a visit to Russian headquarters to present his plan, he was handed over to the Soviet secret police, the NKVD. It is difficult to know what these brutal and suspicious men thought of him – perhaps they thought he was a spy – but they took him to imprisonment in the Soviet Union. When an international storm of protest began demanding his release, the Soviets insisted that he had died in their captivity in 1947, and they maintain this story until this day. However, a number of reports that Wallenberg has been sighted have come out of Russia; there were many well-authenticated reports in the 1950s when many German prisoners-of-war were returning from Soviet captivity, and more sporadic and uncertain claims of meeting him have filtered out since. It seems possible that Wallenberg is still alive and a Soviet prisoner today.

CIVILIANS AND VICTIMS

Of the 50 or 60 million human beings estimated to have been killed as a result of the Second World War, only 17 million or so were in the forces. For almost all the nations involved, "the home front" was no empty phrase. The traditional distinction between those who risked their lives to serve and those who waited at home ceased to have real meaning. In Britain, for instance, until 1942 a serving soldier was more likely to receive a telegram that his wife had been killed by bombing than she was to receive one that he had been killed at the front.

The First World War had been called a war of the masses, but the home countries were still generally comfortable: there was a little bombing, some food shortages, propaganda and some requirement to do war work, but the way of life did not really change, and the greatest fear was that of receiving the black-edged telegram saying that the soldier son was dead. The level of civilian involvement in the Second World War was a new experience; everyone had to be involved. Only a very unusual individual, in very favourable circumstances, could choose to be unaffected (we will meet one such person among the stories here). Middle-class girls who had never worked before joined the women's services or ran the canteens; conscientious objectors and those judged unfit to fight were often given jobs putting them in more danger than serving soldiers. Some countries, such as Germany, established totalitarian terror states to crush any hint of opposition with the threat of execution, while even a democratic country such as Britain resorted to imprisonment without trial and forced labour in the mines.

Possibly the most terrifying experience which civilians had to face was the mass aerial bombing. The justification for this cruel policy was that it would bring enemy populations to submission, destroy enemy economies and be an effective form of retaliation. None of this proved to be the case. In this war of total involvement, the endurance of the masses was never in question, and bombing generated more fighting spirit than it destroyed. In Germany, war production reached its height in 1944 at the same time as the bombing campaign against the country reached its peak. The worst individual bombing was probably the dropping of atom bombs on the Japanese cities of Hiroshima and Nagasaki. In Europe, by far the worst bombing damage was that done to Germany – almost all her cities and most of the smaller towns were devastated. In 1945, the devastated cities were all over Europe: Rotterdam, London, Berlin, Dresden, Warsaw, Leningrad, Stalingrad. So much of Europe's priceless artistic and architectural heritage was destroyed; how lucky we are that Paris, Vienna and Prague survived largely intact to delight future generations as they delighted those of the past.

Even greater horrors than those of mass bombing were reserved for certain groups of civilians: those who experienced the camps. The Jews and Gypsies were the two innocent peoples selected by Hitler and the Nazis for extermination and the extermination camps built in occupied Poland to carry on this ghastly work will be infamous as long as the human race persists. Other populations were called on to bear appalling mass sufferings: after 1945, huge masses of Germans were expelled from their home in eastern Europe with great suffering and loss of life; three million Chinese died, more from general hardship than actual fighting; one-and-a-half million died in the Bengal famine in India in 1943 that might have been prevented had there not been a war on; 20 million civilians and soldiers were lost by Russia.

Just as some were called upon to endure the unendurable, so others escaped lightly. Among the major combatant nations, it was

American civilians who suffered least: no bombs fell at home and the major worry was about sons at the front, 300,000 of whom died. And while the war brought devastation to region after region, in certain areas, such as the Cornwall remembered by Alan Fry, you would hardly have known there was a war being fought at all. It seems a comfort that the greatest conflict mankind has yet devised could leave some, at least, peaceful and unaffected.

Mathilde Wolff-Mönckeberg (1879-1958)

Mathilde Wolff-Mönckeberg was a German civilian who lived through the war in her native city of Hamburg, suffered its terrible destruction by wartime bombing, and recorded the experience with dignity, honesty and humour. She was 60 when the war began and, of her five adult children, four were at that time living either in neutral countries or in countries opposed to Germany. (Her daughter Jacoba was with her in Germany.) During the war she wrote them long, detailed letters, but never sent them. At the beginning of her first letter she explains:

10 October 1940
My beloved far-away children, everything I was not able to tell you in my letters during the first year of the war, was not *allowed* to say, because the censor waited only for an incautious word in order to stop a message from getting through to you, all this I will now put down on paper under the title "Letters that never reached them"; so that much later perhaps you will know what really happened, what we really felt like and why I had to reassure you repeatedly that the "organization" was marvellous, that we were in the best of health and full of confidence. (*On the Other Side*).

As the war went on, she continued writing these letters, often having to stuff the manuscript into a bag as the air-raid warning shrilled yet again, having to keep its existence secret because in the tyrannical Nazi régime any hint of criticism or independent thinking could be made the excuse for imprisonment or even execution. Many years after Mathilde had died, her daughter Ruth (who during the war was living in Wales and later made her home in England) found the letters by accident in a frayed yellow envelope stuffed into an old settle. They have now been published in English with the title *On The Other Side*.

Mathilde Wolff-Mönckeberg, always known to her family as "Tilli", was born on 1 April 1879 into the cultivated, liberal merchant aristocracy of the North German seaports. Her father was lord mayor of Hamburg and knew Bismarck and Brahms.

40 Mathilde Wolf-Mönckeberg with her husband Emil Wolff, her daughter Jacoba Hahn and her grandson Fritz Hahn in April 1946.

Mathilde married two university professors in turn: first André Jolles, from whom she separated and who was the father of her children, and then Emil Wolff, who was professor of English language and literature at Hamburg's university. The couple had only contempt for the Nazi régime which came into power in Germany in 1933. They continued to see their Jewish friends who were now starting to be persecuted, and sometimes (the impulsive and temperamental Mathilde especially) made their feelings plain. But they were lucky enough to be allowed to continue undisturbed.

During the early years of the war, she and her husband suffered, of course, from the absence of their children, but mostly from relatively minor inconveniences such as shortages of some foodstuffs or the transport and other difficulties caused by black-out. Mathilde describes how her friend Frau Schlensog, who sometimes came to visit her in the evening, had to travel home:

10 October 1940
Her return home was horrible, not on account of air-raid warnings like now, which drive visitors home before 9 p.m., but because of her long trek out to Flottbeck during the black-out. She had to wait endlessly for the tram to take her to the main station. On foggy nights vehicles were almost invisible, two shaded red lights announcing the tram gliding through the darkness. The station would swallow her up like a black cavern, and she had to fumble her way down stone steps into an overfull train, lucky to find standing room. On arrival Frau Schlensog still had a twenty-minute walk, often through deep snow. We gave her a small stable lantern with a little red light burning brightly and comfortingly. Thus equipped, her feet in galoshes, her woolly cap drawn right over ears and forehead, she braved many a winter night and told us that often other lonely night-wanderers would join her, attracted by the homely glow of her lamp. She always said she loved the moon, for it made her solitary walk more companionable.

Rarely has our good moon assumed such wide importance as during this first war winter. Everything depended on its gentle light: going to the theatre, going out to dinner, visits to the cinema. Even on cloudy nights one could sense its presence; a brownish, diffused sort of duskiness lay over the streets, never noticed before when there were streetlamps. Nights of full moon and snow have come to mean for me a new source of peace and beauty.

As the years of war went on, the air-raids on Hamburg began, and the routine of jumping out of bed, pulling on a few clothes with trembling fingers, stuffing a few things into a small suitcase and dashing for the lift, began. This daughter of one of Hamburg's leading families, well-meaning as she was, could not quite hide her contempt for the people with whom she was sharing the shelter, people she thought were heedless and naïve in their acceptance of the Nazi regime.

Her husband, Professor Wolff, became ill and had to go into hospital and during 1942 she had to cope with the first deaths in her large and close-knit family: her nephew, First Lieutenant Jasper Mönckeberg, who was killed on the Russian front in February 1942, aged 26 and (her deepest personal sorrow) her son Jan Jolles, who was a Communist in exile in South America and who died of a duodenal ulcer. Sometimes she got news that her grandchildren had been born to one or other of her children abroad, babies she could not hope to see until the war was over.

41 The Mönckebergstrasse in Hamburg, named after Mathilde Wolff-Mönckeberg's family, as it was before the destruction of Hamburg by Allied bombers.

But the greatest test and horror was yet to come. In the early years of the war Hamburg had suffered a fair amoung of bombing, but from 1943 British and American bombers conducted a greatly intensified campaign and in July 1943, Hamburg suffered four of the worst terror raids of the war. These all but destroyed the town, partly by creating vast fire storms in which whole areas with their inhabitants were incinerated. To the Hamburgers, this most terrible few days in their history became known as "the week".

Before the raids, Mathilde Wolff-Mönckeberg noticed the reconnaissance planes coming over night after night, heard the stories of other cities being terribly bombed and read leaflets dropped from the sky saying, "You have got a few weeks' respite, then it will be your turn. There is a peace now, then it will be eternal peace." Here is her description of the first raid on Sunday 25 July:

29 August 1943
Shortly before 1 a.m. the air-raid warning goes. As always we dress in a hurry. But before we even reach the shelter a veritable thunderstorm of noise explodes above us. It doesn't stop for even a second, one detonation following another without respite. The house shakes, the windows tremble and it is completely different from any of the other times. Everybody, including the ailing Frau Hafekin from the first floor, and the Leisers with their baby in its pram, races for the cellar. The light flickers and flickers, but doesn't go out yet. For two whole hours this ear-splitting terror goes on and all you can see is fire. No one speaks. Tense faces wait for the worst at each gargantuan explosion. Heads go down automatically whenever there is a crash and features are trapped in horror. My one thought is: God save Jacoba and Fritz [her daughter remaining in Germany and her grandchild], and make me ready to face the end. At last it gets quieter . . .

The next day, with the whole city shrouded in smoke and the air-raid warnings going off constantly, people began to look for all means to escape the city. An even heavier raid followed on the night of Tuesday/Wednesday, leaving the city with no gas or electricity, no water, no telephones working and no public transport. Mathilde describes the sights to be seen in the worst-hit areas:

24 August, 1943
People who had fled from collapsing bunkers and had got stuck in huge crowds in the streets, had burning phosphorus thrown over them, rushed into the next air-raid shelter and were shot in order not to spread the flames. In the midst of the fire and the attempts to quench it, women had their babies in the streets. Parents and children were separated and torn apart in this frightful upheaval of surging humanity and never found each other again.

In the middle of the terrible conditions, German citizens, many of whom had previously supported the Nazi régime, thought again about the party which has wantonly brought them so much misery:

24 August, 1943
People who were wearing party badges had them torn off their coats and there were screams of "Let's get that murderer"

A general evacuation of women and children began and the Wolffs were out of the town

42 Aerial view of Hamburg after its destruction by Allied bombing.

43 German civilians in a shelter seeking protection from the night raids of the RAF.

before the fourth enormous raid, when their own district received some of the heaviest punishment yet. Incredibly, the house in which their flat was, Andreasstrasse 39, was undamaged, although most of the surrounding area was destroyed.

Now little but ruins, Hamburg continued to be bombed frequently as the years of war went on, although no raids quite so terrible were experienced. As Germany's defeat came closer, conditions deteriorated even further: rations were down to starvation level, electricity cuts were frequent. Photographs of Mathilde Wolff-Mönckeberg show that during the war years she became pathetically

thin and looked like an old woman. During this terrible time, she continued to be sustained by her devotion to her family, her devotion to German literature and music, and her courage.

By April 1945, the end was near:

20 April 1945
And now we have to face the final catastrophe. American troops have advanced as far as Harburg [just outside Hamburg], and the gunfire rolls across our city like thunder. . . . Wherever one looks there are absurd barricades across the streets between heaps of rubble, to be surmounted by little stone steps, which look as if they have been made by children for fun! Are they supposed to keep us safe? Hamburg people laugh and shrug their shoulders.

On 2 May 1945, British soldiers entered Hamburg. The worst ordeals were over, although the people had to face occupation by foreigners, many of whom believed that they were all criminals because their government had been criminal. But Mathilde Wolff-Mönckeberg had reunion with her children and a first sight of many grandchildren to look forward to. She continued to live in her native city of Hamburg until her death in 1958.

Alan Fry (b. 1937)

Alan Fry was born on 15 March 1937, at Kingston-on-Thames near London and, as a child, had his own perception of the war being waged by adults. His father was an electrician and his mother a telephone operator. By the time the war started, the family had moved to Worcester Park in Surrey, on the outskirts of London. His earliest memories concern the war:

The first indication to a three-year-old in 1940

that there was "a war on" was the arrival of several men with spades who dug a large hole in the back garden. I remember a baby bird fell into it and had to be rescued.

The bird trap was in fact a bomb shelter, used mainly at night, which was when "Gerry" in the form of the Heinkels, Messerschmidts and Dorniers of the Luftwaffe came to attack us. These random bombs, sometimes from aircraft under attack by RAF fighters, were not aimed at anything in particular, but for some reason

44 Alan Fry as a child during the war.

frequently hit gas mains, the fires from which often lit the night sky.

When the hole in the garden had been roofed and covered with earth, duck boards installed, and steps and a door fitted, it became a quite regular bedroom for myself, my mother and several neighbours.

As soon as the low moan of the air-raid warning rose to its familiar howl, mother gathered up our bedding, thrust a chamber pot into my hands, and we trooped off under ground. The chamber pot was most essential – no lavatory in the shelter.

Usually the raid was taking place miles away and I would stand at the door of the shelter watching the search lights probing the blackness. Most of the time, close to the door was the best place to be. The shelter had no proper ventilation, and when four people were in it the air became foul.

In a London suburb, life continued much as usual for a growing child. Some types of food and items of clothing were in short supply and could only be bought in exchange for coupons printed in official ration books. Bananas were

45 Garden shelter being tested out at Hornchurch, Essex.

not available at all until after 1945, and Alan Fry remembers asking what the long yellow things advertised on the old Fyffes posters were and why there were none available: he received the usual answer, a catchphrase of the war, "Don't you know there's a war on?" This was the blanket excuse for any shortage or inconvenience.

There was a great deal of queueing during and shortly after the war. People were keen to get their share of whatever was going, and it became quite a joke that some would join any queue simply to see what was at the end of it. Alan Fry remembers hearing the story of a woman who had stood in a queue, with a shopping bag for half an hour when she asked the person next to her what they were queuing for. "Tales of Hoffman," came the answer. "Really," said the woman, "How do you cook them?"

46 Children being evacuated from London.

aware of the radio news coverage of the war and heard the Luftwaffe raids on the Vickers aircraft factory nearby. When Vickers was "getting it", he and his classmates were herded into the air-raid shelters for fear the school might be mistaken for part of the Vickers workshops.

The Vickers factory was busily engaged in turning out aircraft that would be used to bomb Germany and cause her, in the latter stages of the war, infinitely more destruction than even Britain had suffered. Alan Fry comments on this:

There was no remorse about indiscriminate bombing – not yet. Germans, it was taken for granted, were the embodiment of everything evil. They had started the bombing of ordinary people, and it was only just that they too were now being killed. It mattered not at all whether they were civilians or service people.

The same went for the Japanese. Indeed, when the news came that Hiroshima and Nagasaki had been atom-bombed, there was nothing but rejoicing. The Japanese were, like the Germans, the enemy and therefore killing them was "a good thing". The American airmen who had slaughtered so many with their atomic bombs were the toast of Britain.

The Japanese were hated with a fervour even the Germans had escaped. When the emaciated victims of their prisoner-of-war-camps started arriving home, the feeling, if anything, began to get worse. The films we saw of German concentration camps had involved mostly foreigners, but many of the victims of Japan had been British.

The war may have been fought to defend democracy, or defeat fascism, or from any number of high-minded motives, but its most lasting effect on young minds was an abiding distrust of the Germans and Japanese. Few of the children who experienced the war will ever entirely free themselves of it.

Eventually the German air-raids became so intense that many children were evacuated to remote rural districts. Many were sent to total strangers, who might not be very willing to receive them, but Alan Fry was luckier: he went with his mother to Pendoggett in north Cornwall to stay with a succession of friends and relatives, while his father stayed at home to work.

What struck the growing Alan Fry there was how remote the war seemed. Apart from the absence of his father and hearing such news as that local young men, mainly in the Merchant Navy, had been killed, he remembers that: "Cornwall could have been as neutral as Switzerland". There were no air bases, no air-raids, and even rationing was less of a problem than it had been in Worcester Park: there was little difficulty obtaining eggs and meat, as most people in Cornwall, as in rural England generally, kept animals – pigs, chickens and rabbits.

Gradually, the bombing of Britain eased off, and Alan Fry went to live at New Haw near Weybridge in Surrey. Here he became

In 1944, Alan Fry remembers, the road outside the school was blocked, for days on end, by military traffic. A seemingly endless procession of lorries, armoured cars and Bren gun carriers were rumbling their way to the

47 A mobile refreshment van giving out food and tea to Air Raid Precautions (ARP) workers and bombed-out civilians after a flying bomb raid on London. •

south. D-Day, the invasion of the European continent via Normandy by the British and Americans, was soon under way. Victory for the Allies was less than a year away. But the British public was in for another reminder that this was a war on the home front too. The Germans now launched their dreaded secret weapons, first the V1, a kind of rocket-propelled, unmanned aircraft packed with high explosive, and, later, the deadly V2: this was a true rocket, the forerunner of today's inter-continental missiles. It struck without warning, giving its victims no chance.

Most V2s were aimed at London, but far from their creating blind terror among the inhabitants of the city, people went about their business much as if there was nothing happening. Indeed, there were no special precautions to take. Alan Fry remembers, as a small child, being taken into London by train, and that people were more worried by the endless train delays which were common in wartime than by the risk of bombs. There were often foreign servicemen on the trains, particularly American GIs. He remembers sharing a compartment once with a party of black GIs. There were only a few black people living in England then, and Alan Fry was astounded to see for the first time people of another colour.

Another foreign contact during those years was a family of Belgian refugees, the Lepères,

48 Britain celebrates victory in 1945.

whom Alan Fry's family had taken in and who lived in half their house. They had left Belgium when the Germans arrived. Alan remembers they spoke sometimes in Flemish and sometimes in French, and tried to teach him French. He also remembers that they did not seem very grateful for the accommodation that had been offered them.

Alan Fry was in London when the Germans surrendered. He remembers VE Day:

Crowds swarmed on to the streets. Servicemen were mobbed, and I well remember a policeman being tossed high in the air – and caught, I may add – by a crowd of excited revellers. It was a day of unrestrained joy.

These spontaneous celebrations were followed within a day or two by street parties of the kind which marked the Queen's recent Silver Jubilee or the Royal Wedding of 1981. There was an immense sense of a great and historic victory.

Alan Fry was eight-and-a-half years old when the war ended. Since then, he has gone on to become a successful journalist.

Julian Maclaren-Ross (1912-1964)

In a great modern war, almost all citizens in the nations that are fighting find that their personal lives become subordinated to the national purpose. But wars also offer opportunities to certain defiant, outstanding individuals, either to distinguish themselves with acts of individual daring and enterprise in the national service, or, more rarely, to set themselves up against the machine, to refuse to allow their individual needs to be subsumed in war, to flourish in a secret half-world of their own. An individual of the latter type was Julian Maclaren-Ross.

With his dark green glasses, silver-knobbled stick, long cigarette-holder, white crimplene suit and teddy-bear coat, and speaking incessantly in a high nasal drawl, Maclaren-Ross became a familiar figure during the war in the pubs, clubs and eating-places of central London, where writers and artists mixed with servicemen on leave and members of the underworld. He was a formidable bohemian who, although usually broke, always travelled by taxi because it is less easy for someone to serve a writ on you there than if you travel by public transport. Thought by many to be a bore or a rogue,

Maclaren-Ross has left us, in his *Memoirs of the Forties* and his wartime short stories, an amusing and accurate record of the war years.

Julian Maclaren-Ross was born in 1912 in South Norwood in London, the son of middle-class parents who were usually short of money. In the 1930s, Julian worked for a while as a vacuum-cleaner salesman for Hoover and Electrolux, and then with a friend

49 Julian Maclaren-Ross, caustic observer of wartime London.

formed a project of looking after people's gardens, "a subject about which they knew nothing", as a friend, the poet Alan Ross, has remarked. Looking after one particular garden landed them in the County Court charged with wilful damage. During this time, Maclaren-Ross had begun to write his short stories.

In 1940 Maclaren-Ross was conscripted into the army, and he tells us in *Memoirs of the Forties:*

"They can do anything to you in the army bar give you a baby," the old London-Irish porter who'd had varicocele and served in four campaigns told me as I got aboard the train in July 1940. "But keep your trap shut and your bowels open you can't come to no harm."

So I reported as ordered to the Infantry Training camp at Blandford, Essex, and was there enlisted as No. 6027033 Private Ross J.

Maclaren-Ross was to prove notably incompetent at following the advice to keep his "trap shut". He was a private soldier, but it was obvious that he was not quite as other privates: he had already had short stories accepted by the wartime literary magazine *Horizon*, founded by the man-of-letters Cyril Connolly who did so much to encourage young writers, and this was at a time when literature was written almost exclusively by the officer class. Officers with literary aspirations kept asking to meet him, although fraternization between the ranks was severely frowned on. His eccentricity gained him a reputation for troublemaking among his immediate superiors. Perhaps the thing to do with him was to make him into an officer?

But his efforts to become an officer were foiled when at the War Office Selection Board Exam he decided to blow up a bridge over an imaginary chasm and "save the lives of my men at the expense of my own". As he did this, he shouted "BOOM" to simulate the sound of the explosion, and this apparently convinced the examiners that he was not serious officer material.

During his brief army career, Maclaren-Ross did not see much action, although his army base was the subject of several raids from German bombers and one direct hit. Eventually he went absent without leave,

50 The lively scene in Fitzrovia in 1942: Osbert Lancaster's cartoon for the wartime magazine *Horizon* edited by Cyril Connolly.

51 "The Wheatsheaf" in Rathbone Place, London –
the pub where Julian Maclaren Ross spent many an
evening as the flying bombs fell.

Wheatsheaf" in Rathbone Place (a pub that remains largely unchanged today, although the once lively area has become quiet). Among those who drank here were no fewer than three writers, Maclaren-Ross included, who had been invalided out of the army on psychiatric grounds. The writer Robert Hewison describes others who might turn up on this scene:

Others found their literary talents shifted them to London jobs with the Army Education Corps or Intelligence. These mixed with Conscientious Objectors, the militarily unemployable, prostitutes, con-men, gangsters, and students not yet called up (known collectively as "The Slithy Toves" because of their alleged resemblance to Tenniel's illustrations to *Alice*). The atmosphere was dense with tobacco smoke and alcohol, sometimes exploding into fights and always noisy with argument. The artist Nina Hamnett might appear rattling her money box – "*My dear*, could you advance me a quid? There's the most beautiful GI passed out stone cold and naked as a duck in my kitchen". (*Under Seige*)

Among other eccentrics moving around the scene were the Countess Eileen Duveen, who had been cured of drug addiction and lived on cream puffs, and the Count Potocki de Montalk, who claimed to be the rightful king of Poland and peddled copies of his own right-wing newspaper, but who was unkindly rumoured really to be an Australian. Young men on leave from the forces, such as the poet Alan Ross who was serving with the Baltic convoys to Russia, added a touch of respectability and a reminder of wartime.

Maclaren-Ross's friend Dan Davin describes the routine Maclaren-Ross lived as part of this literary bohemia:

Midday in the pub until closing time, a late lunch at the Scala restaurant in Charlotte Street, a stroll to look at the bookshops in the Charing Cross

spent some time in a tough army prison (the Glasshouse), was court-martialled, sent to a psychiatric hospital and invalided out of the army as unfit to serve.

For the rest of the war Maclaren-Ross worked in a documentary film unit, where one of his colleagues was the great Welsh poet Dylan Thomas, who had been rejected as physically unfit for military service. Outside working hours, the two men became fixtures of the wartime literary bohemia centred on the pubs of Soho and Fitzrovia, particularly "The

52 Nina Hamnett, the artist who was a great feature of wartime Fitzrovia, pictured in her local.

were being killed. Nevertheless, it was the war that had made this lifestyle possible. The war created the market for Maclaren-Ross's writing, brought him to the height of his modest fame and gave him his subject-matter. The war created the particular circle around the pubs of Soho and Fitzrovia (afterwards, it was to break up, and although Maclaren-Ross continued to go to "The Wheatsheaf", he was often heard to ask where everyone had got to). The 1950s were a "decade I could have done without", his writing increasingly forgotten and bands of creditors often gathering outside the offices where he was picking up freelance work. He died, still impoverished and pursued, still travelling by taxi, in 1964.

Shortly before he died he wrote the first half of *Memoirs of the Forties*, the book which has done so much to fix the legend of wartime literary London. It was the historical moment in which he had been born to live. His friend Dan Davin sums up this feeling:

Road and to buy Royalty, his special jumbo-sized cigarettes. Opening time again at the Wheatsheaf till closing time. A hurried dash to the Highlander, which closed half an hour later. Back to the Scala for supper and coffee. At midnight the tube home from Goodge Street. (*Closing Times*)

All these hours Maclaren-Ross would talk incessantly to whoever would listen or pretend to listen. When he got home he wrote his amusing and realistic short stories about army life. It was a lifestyle that seemed to be based on entirely ignoring the war in which millions

Blackout, ration books, clothing coupons, spivs and rackets, shortage of spirits and even of beer, black-market restaurants and exigiuous steaks, cigarettes hard to get and in flimsy paper packets, the flying bomb and the V2 going bump in the night, *Penguin New Writing, Horizon* and its Begging Bowl – all these return half-credible when I think of the time I first came to know Julian Maclaren-Ross. (*Closing Times*)

Olga Lengyel

Of all the crimes committed against humanity during the Second World War, none was so terrible as the attempt made by the Nazi régime in Germany to exterminate all the Jews of Europe for no other reason than that they were Jews. It is difficult to say which is more horrific: the methodical, ruthless cruelty with which the deed was carried out or the

perverted and senseless state of mind which allowd men to conceive such a plan. The Nazi attempts at forming an ideology to justify this mass-murder – the belief that the Germans constituted the cream of the Aryan race of "superhumans" while the Jews could be classified as "non-human" and therefore not fit to live – was pathetic in its lack of science.

The names of the extermination camps with gas chambers which the Nazis set up – Auschwitz, Treblinka, Maidanek and the others – will never be forgotten. A few victims survived to tell the world of the sufferings endured by millions, and among these was Olga Lengyel.

Olga Lengyel and her family were among the hundreds of thousands of Jews living in Hungary outside Budapest, the last major group of Jews to fall victim to Nazi terror, in 1944. She lived in Cluj, where her husband, Miklos Lengyel, was the director of his own hospital, "Doctor Lengyel's Sanitorium". Olga also worked in the hospital as his chief surgical assistant. They had two sons, Thomas and Arvad, and in their house also lived Olga's parents, and her godfather, Elfer Aladar, a distinguished man in the field of cancer research. They were the sort of cultivated, prosperous, close-knit Jewish family which was once so common all over central and eastern Europe.

During the early years of the war, the family heard many stories of the enormities committed against the Jews in occupied Europe. They gave shelter to refugees although they did not believe that such stories could be true. Then, during the first week in May 1944, the Germans began a partial occupation of Hungary. Dr Lengyel was summoned to the police station and told he was to be deported to Germany immediately, to be sent away within the hour. Olga Lengyel decided that her destiny was with her husband, and her parents, having tried in vain to dissuade her, finally decided to accompany her. Nor could she leave her children behind.

The Germans had lied: the destination of the train was not Germany but Auschwitz, the extermination camp in German-annexed Poland. When they Lengyels reached the station in a taxi, they discovered that scores of friends and neighbours were there too. A long train was waiting, but not composed of passenger coaches, only cattle cars. They were pushed into a train, and when the door was shut, 96 men, women and children had been packed into a space intended for eight horses. They were on the train for eight days; the atmosphere grew poisonous, they were given no food beyond what they had brought, and only tiny amounts of water were brought to them. Many died, but they were not allowed to remove the bodies.

When they arrived at Auschwitz, they were lined up in groups of five, men and women separate. They were paraded before about 30 SS men, including the camp commandant. Unknown to them, this was the first "selection" by which those to be gassed and burned immediately in the crematories were chosen. Children, the aged and the infirm were sent to the left, which was to mean immediate extermination; the able-bodied were sent to the right, which was to mean a period of hard labour before being killed. Olga Lengyel describes this moment for her family:

Our turn came. My mother, my sons, and I stepped before the "selectors". The selector waved my mother and myself to the adult group. He classed my younger son Thomas with the children and aged, which was to mean immediate extermination. He hesitated before Arvad, my older son.

My heart thumped violently. The officer, a large dark man who wore glasses, seemed to be trying to act fairly. . . . "This boy must be more than twelve," he remarked to me.

"No," I protested.

The truth was that Arvad was not quite twelve . . . he was big for his age, but I wanted to spare him from labours that might prove too arduous for him.

"Very well, . . . to the left."

I persuaded my mother that she should follow the children and take care of them. . . . He again acquiesced. "You'll all be in the same camp."

"And in several weeks you'll all be reunited," another officer added, with a smile. "Next!"
(Olga Lengyel, *Five Chimneys*)

Olga Lengyel believed that, in her desire to spare her elder son and mother from back-breaking work, she had become partly responsible for their death; this terrible sense of guilt was one of the worst things she had to bear.

The *blocova* ("barrack chief") in her

barrack informed her of what would have happened to her family. They would have been marched from Auschwitz camp itself, which was the work camp, to the nearby camp of Birkenau, where the gas chambers and crematory ovens were situated. There they would have been told to undress completely under the pretext that they were to take a shower and packed into a low, narrow hall. Then the poisonous gas, Zyklon-B, would have been released from above into the chamber. After the sufferers had died in agony, they would have been taken from the chamber and their bodies shovelled into the crematory ovens. The crematory chimneys, of which there were five, gave out a sweetish odour of burning human flesh which pervaded the whole camp of Auschwitz-Birkenau.

Olga's own fate was terrible enough. Like all other prisoners, she was shaved and given rags to wear. The *Lager* (camp) occupied a vast space of about six to eight miles, guarded by watch posts and electrified barbed wire. Inside, the prisoners lived in wooden cages called *koias*; each cage measured 12 x 15 feet and housed up to 20 people who slept on bare boards or, if they were lucky, with one filthy blanket among ten. Sanitary and other provisions were virtually non-existent, and the roofs often leaked, exposing the inmates to every weather. The 1500 women in Olga Lengyel's barrack were given 20 bowls for their meagre food (bread mixed with sawdust and filthy-smelling soup), but the woman chosen to be *blocova* and her cronies immediately commandeered these as chamber pots. The other women were allowed to visit the latrines twices a day; if they went out during the night, they would be shot by the SS.

The most important ceremonies in the camp were the daily "roll calls". Here the prisoners, dressed in their rags, had to remain standing in front of their barracks for many hours in all weathers. The sick had to be present at the roll call, and even those who had died in the barrack, their bodies propped up by their fellows. Many prisoners died of cold and exhaustion during roll call. Sometimes further victims for the gas chamber were

53 The so-called "Gate of Death" leading to the crematory at the extermination camp of Birkenau.

selected. The SS women, Hasse and Griese, and the camp doctors, Mengele and Klein, normally carried out these selections (all these were hanged after the war, except Dr Josef Mengele, the chief selector, who escaped and may only recently have died. Twenty to 40 persons were taken each time, chosen at random by the selectors. One of the SS women, the 22-year-old Irma Griese, was of very great beauty; it was said she chose good-looking women to die, being jealous of any competition. Dr Mengele sometimes made the women parade in front of him, naked, with their hands in the air; in some unknown way, this enabled him to select his victims. Sometimes whole sections of the camp were

54 The crematorium furnaces at Auschwitz-Birkenau and the carts on which corpses were delivered there.

55 In one of the women's barracks at the Auschwitz concentration camp in 1945.

exterminated. Czech prisoners held in a special "Czech camp" were treated relatively favourably for a time and then learnt that they were to be liquidated immediately:

That afternoon a Czech boy, who was in love with a young *Vertreterin* (*blocova's* lieutenant) from our camp, said goodbye to her through the barbed wire that separated us. He knew how the day would end for him.

"When you see the first flames from the crematory at daybreak," he said, "you will know that it is my greeting to you."

The girl fainted. He gazed at her through the barbed wire with tears in his eyes. We helped her to get up.

"Dear," he continued, "I have a diamond that I wanted to give you as a present. I stole it while I was working in Canada [the storeroom where prisoners' belongings were kept before being sent to Germany]. But now I shall try to exchange it for a chance to go over to your camp to be with you before I die."

It was somehow arranged, and the boy came over. . . . The *blocova* left the young people alone in her room. The other inmates stood outside to watch for the Germans. (*Five Chimneys*)

That night trucks arrived at the "Czech camp" to take the inmates to the gas chambers. The SS ran their hooked poles through all who tried to resist. The young *Vertreterin* watched her Czech lover being pushed into the truck and saw the smoke rising from the crematory chimney at dawn; during the night, her hair turned white.

The Nazis' intention was eventually to exterminate all the Jews in Auschwitz, after having subjected them to a period of hard work first, useful to the German economy. The work the Jews had to do during their period of waiting was usually harsh and degrading: carrying stones up and down hill, clearing latrines and so on. Olga Lengyel was luckier than most in that her medical skills eventually brought her work in the camp infirmary and slightly better conditions of life. Olga was able to help the sick and became involved in the camp resistance, whose work consisted of passing on forbidden information, stealing from the Germans and acts of sabotage. Sometimes there were attempts at revolt in the camp, but these were always brutally crushed.

When, towards the end of 1944, it was clear that the Russians were closing in on Poland, the gas chambers and crematories ceased to function. But the Germans, found a cheap and efficient alternative method of disposing of the children who had somehow managed to escape the initial selection. Olga Lengyel describes how she and other prisoners were made to "bathe" the children in outdoor showers in snowy weather, and then they were made to stand at "roll call" in the snow. Almost all died of exposure, and those who survived were cudgelled to death.

56 Survivors of the Auschwitz-Birkenau extermination camp gathered on the site of Birkenau on 27 January, 1985, the anniversary of the liberation of the camp.

Finally, orders came to evacuate the camp and, on the march westwards, fleeing from the advancing Russian soldiers, Olga Lengyel eventually managed to escape. Her book, *Five Chimneys*, bears witness to the atrocities of Auschwitz and other camps like it.

Dr Michihiko Hachiya

Today it is difficult to contemplate the dropping of atom bombs on the Japanese cities of Hiroshima and Nagasaki and the subsequent suffering caused by atomic radiation – the burning and vapourization of human beings and the pain and deaths from radiation sickness going on years after the event. But that was not entirely how it seemed at the time. To the Americans who made the decision to drop the bomb, it was simply another bomb, much larger than earlier ones of course, but no different in kind. The dropping of the bombs helped to bring the war with Japan to a speedy end. It was argued that this saved the need for a bloody invasion of Japan with, perhaps, a million casualties. People over the Western World were stunned by the news that atom bombs had been dropped, but they rejoiced that the war was over and that prisoners were coming home. Only later, when the facts of radiation injury became horribly clear, and when it had become possible to make bombs a million times more destructive than those that pulverized these unfortunate cities, did Hiroshima and Nagasaki come to see a uniquely awful warning to mankind.

Dr Michihiko Hachiya, director of the Hiroshima Communications Hospital, was one of the Japanese who lived through the bombing of Hiroshima. Badly injured, he recovered enough to take up his work as a doctor helping others even more badly hurt than himself, to ponder what had happened and to write about these events. He wrote a diary covering the period from 6 August 1945,

57 The type of atom bomb detonated over Hiroshima. It is 28in. in diameter, 120in. long, weighs about 9000 pounds and has a yield equivalent to about 20,000 tons of explosive.

the day the atom bomb was dropped on Hiroshima, to 30 September, after the Japanese surrender had been signed. It was later published as *Hiroshima Diary*.

On the night before the explosion, Dr Hachiya had been working until 4 a.m. as an air-raid warden at his hospital. He came home and went to sleep on the living-room floor of his home, which was a few hundred metres from the hospital. At 7 a.m. the air-raid warning went, but it was followed by the all-clear at 8 a.m. Dr Hachiya dozed. Later, he wrote in his diary:

Suddenly a strong flash of light startled me – and then another. . . . The view where a moment before all had been so bright and sunny was now dark and hazy. Through swirling dust I could barely discern a wooden column that had supported one corner of my house. It was leaning crazily and the roof sagged dangerously. Moving instinctly, I tried to escape, but rubble and fallen timbers barred the way.... A profound weakness overcame me. . . . To my surprise I discovered that I was completely naked. . . . What had happened?

All over the right side of my body I was cut and bleeding. A large splinter was protruding from a mangled wound in my thigh, and something warm trickled into my mouth. . . . Embedded in my neck was a sizable fragment of glass. . . .

Badly injured as he was, Dr Hachiya was much better off than people closer to the hypocentre of the explosion (Dr Hachiya's house was about 1600 metre from the hypocentre: within 500 metres almost nothing and no one had survived. 71,000 people had been killed instantaneously by the power of atomic fission.) Dr Hachiya's wife was also badly burned (their ten-year-old son was luckily with Dr Hachiya's mother in the country, having been sent there for safety) and their house had been entirely destroyed. They made their way painfully towards Dr Hachiya's hospital. On arrival a fire broke out in the hospital, and Dr Hachiya and some staff were evacuated into the garden where they were almost burnt to death. He fainted, and when he woke heavy raindrops laden with radioactive dust were falling. All around lay dead bodies and the fires burned in the ruins of the city.

When the explosion had happened, there had been no patients in the hospital because Dr Hachiya, fearing there might be trouble in still-unbombed Hiroshima, had evacuated them to the country. But now patients with terrible burns, severe injuries, vomiting and bleeding began to besiege the hospital, although there were no resources to treat them. Of 190 doctors in Hiroshima at the time of the explosion, 72 had been killed and others were injured. Dr Hachiya had to lie in bed amid the dirt and disorder for several days feeling helpless and guilty that he could not do more as a doctor.

Various friends came to visit him, and one told him:

Between the Red Cross Hospital and the centre of the city I saw nothing that wasn't burned. . . . Tramcars were standing . . . and inside were dozens of bodies, blackened beyond recognition. I saw fire reservoirs filled to the brim with dead people who looked as if they had been boiled alive. In one reservoir I saw a man,

58 Devastation at Hiroshima after the atom bomb — some reinforced concrete buildings escaped total destruction; elsewhere only deformed trees, stripped of their foliage, mark where buildings once were.

horribly burned, crouching beside another man who was dead. He was drinking blood-stained water out of the reservoir . . . he was completely out of his head. In one reservoir there were so many dead people there wasn't enough room for them to fall over. They must have died sitting in the water.

Conditions within the hospital were pitiful enough:

There were no radios, no electric lights, not even a candle. The only light that came to me was reflected in flickering shadows made by the burning city. The only sounds were the groans and sobs of the patients. Now and then a patient in delirium would call for his mother, or the voice of one in pain would breathe out the word *eraiyo* – "the pain is unbearable; I cannot endure it!"

As the days passed, Dr Hachiya was able to get up and take part in the running of the hospital, also to go around Hiroshima and try to find out what had happened. There were no newspapers and no radio in the city and it was not known at first what sort of bomb had caused so much damage. There were rumours that there was poisonous gas around Hiroshima, and that the city would be uninhabitable for the next 75 years. Panic-stricken people wanted to flee. Dr Hachiya tried to quell these rumours, but other terrible facts were beginning to become plain. At first, it was thought patients who had not been too terribly burned and seemed to be getting better would continue to do so. But this proved not to be true. With horror, and yet as a doctor trying to understand what was happening, Dr Hachiya watched the progress of the "radiation sickness". Patients began to lose their hair, they developed boils or *petechiae* on their skin, fevers, bloody stools and vomiting, and most died within days or weeks. (What was not known when Dr Hachiya wrote his diary was that people would continue to fall ill with diseases related to contaminated nuclear fallout for years after the event.) Dr Hachiya noted that the nearer a patient was to the hypocentre at the time of the explosion, the more likely he or she was to develop radiation sickness. He grabbed some of his own hair and pulled.

I did not have much hair in the first place, but the amount that came out made me feel sick.

Gradually, the number of people dying each day started to decrease a little, and people began to take comfort in small things such as supplies of bowls and dishes at the hospital and the resumption of the post and electric light again. On 15 August the Japanese emperor Hirohito announced the capitulation of Japan in a broadcast: the atom bombs on Hiroshima and Nagasaki, and Russia's intervention in the war against Japan, had finally made the Japanese surrender. But, in spite of what they had suffered, many Japanese wanted to continue with the war.

59 Burns of an atom bomb victim reproduce the pattern of the dark patches on a kimono worn at the time of the explosion.

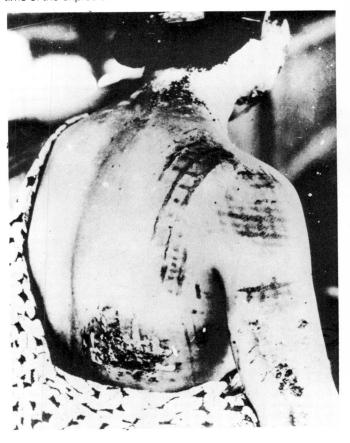

60 The "mushroom cloud" billowing 20,000 feet over the doomed Japanese city of Nagasaki after the atomic attack.

The emperor's words filled the ward with despair and desperation. People shouted "Only a coward would back out now!", "What have we been suffering for?" and "Those who died can't go to heaven in peace now!"

The capitulation, however, had to be accepted as did the presence of occupying American troops, whom the people of Hiroshima, perhaps strangely, seemed to accept with little resentment. The Americans now offered help and friendship and did not humiliate the proud Japanese. But again and again people's minds turned towards the terrible and inexplicable thing that had happened to them, which had left scarcely a family with no members dead or horribly injured. The total number who died will never be known, but it is thought to be around 250,000, more than half the population of the city. A friend of Dr Hachiya's had been outside the city and seen the mushroom cloud, which he said was neither red nor yellow and "beautiful beyond description". When he had gone, Dr Hachiya reflected:

I had, of course, heard people say the sky was beautiful. . . but it was now, for the first time, that I could picture the cloud sharply defined against a clear blue August sky. It was at the moment of the birth of this cloud, with its ever-changing colour, that Hiroshima was wiped out. It was at this moment that Hiroshima city, the culmination of many years' work, disappeared with her good citizens into the beautiful sky.

DATE LIST

1931
September — Japanese overrun Manchuria, signalling attack on China.

1932
August — Chinese Communists declare war on Japan in name of Kiangsi Soviet.

1933
January — Hitler becomes German chancellor with wide-ranging expansion programme.

1934
February — Civil war almost breaks out in France.

1935
September — Nürnberg laws in Germany take away citizenship from Jews.

1936
March — Germany re-occupies the Rhineland.
May — Ethiopian resistance to Italians collapses.
October — Rome-Berlin Axis formed between Hitler and Mussolini.

1937
July — Second and more intense phase of Sino-Japanese war begins.

1938
March — Hitler's Germany takes over Austria.
September — Munich conference marks German triumph in Czechoslovakia.

1939
March — Hitler takes over Czechoslovakia, and British and French governments guarantee security of Poland.
May — Hitler tells his generals war over Poland is "inevitable".
August — Hitler and Stalin sign Nazi/Soviet pact.
1 September — Germany invades Poland and annexes Danzig.
3 September — Britain, France, Australia and New Zealand declare war on Germany.
29 September — Russia and Germany sign agreement partioning Poland.
30 November — Russia invades Finland.

1940
12 March — Russo-Finnish pact signed.
9 April — Germany invades Denmark and Norway.
10 May — Germany launches main attack in West. Churchill becomes British prime minister.
14 June — Germans enter Paris as conquerors.
10 July – 15 September — Battle of Britain saves Britain from invasion.
4 August — Italians invade British and French Somaliland.

14 September — Italians invade Egypt.
28 October — Italians invade Greece.

1941
6 April — Germans invade Yugoslavia and Greece.
13 April — Non-aggression pact signed between Japan and Russia.
5 May — Haile Selassie enters Addis Ababa in triumph.
20 May — Germans take Crete from British.
22 June — Germans invade the Soviet Union.
17 August — Kiev falls to Germans.
6 December — Russian counter-offensive near Moscow begins.
7 December — Japanese attack on American fleet at Pearl Harbor.
11 December — Germany and Italy declare war on the United States.

1942
15 February — Japanese capture Singapore from British.
30 May — First "1000 bomber" raid on German city of Köln.
3-4 June — Battle of Midway marks turning point of Pacific war.
13 September — Battle for Stalingrad begins.
23 October — Battle of El Alamein begins.
3-5 November — Axis troops begin to retreat from El Alamein.

1943
23 January — British Eighth army enters Tripoli.
2 February — Germans surrender at Stalingrad.
8 February — Wingate's Chindits make first expedition into Burma.
18 April — Yamamoto shot down by American air force.
19 April — Jewish uprising in Warsaw Ghetto begins.
13 May — Germans and Italians surrender in Tunisia.
4 July — Battle of Kursk begins.
9-10 July — Allied invasion of Sicily begins.
25 July — Mussolini is imprisoned.
8 September — Italians announce surrender and Germans move to occupy Rome.
1 October — Fifth army captures Naples.
18 November — Heaviest air attacks yet on German capital Berlin.

1944
22 January — Allies establish the bridgehead at Anzio.
29 March — Siege of Imphal begins.
2 April — Russians enter Romania.
4 June — Rome falls to the Allies.
6 June — D-day invasion of Normandy beaches begins.
20 July — The bomb plot against Hitler fails.
1 August — Warsaw rising against Germans begins.
24 August — Paris is liberated.
31 August — Budapest is liberated.
17 September — Allied operation at Arnhem begins.
2 October — Warsaw patriots capitulate to the Germans.

14 October	Athens is liberated.
20 October	Belgrade is liberated.

1945

17 January	Warsaw is liberated.
13/14 February	Dresden is bombed, Budapest is liberated.
6 March	Allies take Köln.
13 April	Belsen and Buchenwald concentration camps are liberated.
28 April	Mussolini is killed by Italian partisans.
30 April	Hitler commits suicide while Russians take Berlin.
8 May	Final capitulation of Germany signed.
13 May	Russian occupation of Czechoslovakia ends European fighting.
6 August	Atom bomb is dropped on Hiroshima.
8 August	Russia declares war on Japan.
14 August	Japanese agree on unconditional surrender.
2 September	Japanese surrender signed.

BOOKS FOR FURTHER READING

General Histories of the War

M. Arnold-Forster, *The World at War*, Associated Book Publishers, 1981

P. Calvocoressi & C. Wint, *Total War*, Pelican, 1972

A.J.P. Taylor, *The Second World War*, Penguin, 1976

General Studies of the War

M. Baudot, Henri Bernard *et al* (eds.), *The Historical Encyclopaedia of World War II*, Macmillan, 1981

J. Keegan (ed.) *Who was Who in World War II*, Arms and Armour Press, 1978

D. Mason, *Who's Who in World War II*, Weidenfeld & Nicholson, 1978

T. Parrish (ed.), *The Encyclopaedia of World War II*, Secker & Warburg, 1978

C. Tunney, *Biographical Dictionary of World War II*, Dent, 1972

Particular Aspects of the War

J. Ellis, *The Sharp End of War*, David & Charles, 1980

M.R.D. Foot, *Resistance*, Eyre Methuen, 1976

M.R.D. Foot, *SOE 1940-46*, BBC Publications, 1984

N.L. Fyson, *Growing Up in the Second World War*, B.T. Batsford, 1979

M. Gilbert, *Final Journey*, Allen & Unwin, 1979

C.A.R. Hills, *The Fascist Dictatorships*, B.T. Batsford, 1979

F. Huggett, *Goodnight Sweetheart*, W.H. Allen, 1979

R. Jackson, *Fighter Pilots of World War II*, Arthur Barker, 1976

N. Longmate, *How We Lived Then*, Hutchinson, 1971

R. Parkinson, *The Origins of World War II*, Wayland, 1976

R. Parkinson, *Attack on Pearl Harbour*, Wayland, 1973

T. Prittie, *Germans Against Hitler*, Hutchinson, 1964

H. Rumpf, *The Bombing of Germany*, Frederick Muller, 1963

A.J.P. Taylor, *The War Lords*, Hamish Hamilton, 1977

H. Trevor Roper, *The Last Days of Hitler*, Pan, 1972

M. Yass, *Hiroshima*, Wayland, 1971

Personal Accounts, Biographies and War Adventures

R.S. Abib Jr, *Here We Are Together*, Longman, 1946

A. Bull, *Anne Frank*, Hamish Hamilton, 1984

A. Bullock, *Hitler: a Study in Tyranny*, Pelican, 1962

G. Clare, *Last Waltz in Vienna*, Macmillan, 1981

A. Donat, *The Holocaust Kingdom*, Secker & Warburg, 1965

P. Harcourt, *The Real Enemy*, Longman, 1976

R. Hillary, *The Last Enemy*, Pan, 1969

C.A.R. Hills, *The Hitler File*, B.T. Batsford, 1980

J. Verney, *Going to the Wars*, Anthony Mott, 1983

E. Williams, *The Wooden Horse*, Penguin, 1984

Books By and About People Featured in this Book

J. Bierman, *Righteous Gentile*, Allen Lane, 1981

O.P. Chaney Jr, *Zhukov*, David & Charles, 1972

D. Davin, *Closing Times*, Oxford University Press, 1975

K. Douglas, *Alamein to Zem Zem*, Oxford University Press, 1971

The Complete Poems of Keith Douglas (ed. Desmond Graham), Oxford University Press, 1978

J.O. Fuller, *Madeleine*, Gollancz, 1952

D. Graham, *Keith Douglas 1920-1944*, Oxford University Press, 1974

M. Hachiya, *Hiroshima Diary*, Gollancz, 1952

R. Hewison, *Under Siege*, Weidenfeld & Nicholson, 1977

O. Lengyel, *Five Chimneys*, Granada, 1972

J. Maclaren Ross, *Memoirs of the Forties*, Penguin, 1984

A. Mockler, *Haile Selassie's War*, Oxford University Press, 1984

L. Mosley, *Haile Selassie*, Weidenfeld & Nicholson, 1964

F. Mowat, *And No Birds Sang*, Anthony Mott, 1984

J.D. Potter, *Admiral of the Pacific*, Heinemann, 1965

F. von Schlabrendorff, *Revolt against Hitler*, Eyre & Spottiswood, 1948

F. von Schlabrendorff, *The Secret War against Hitler*, Hodder & Stoughton, 1966

M. Wolff-Mönckeberg, (ed. Ruth Evans) *On the Other Side*, Peter Owen, 1979

The Memoirs of Marshal Zhukov, Jonathan Cape, 1971

INDEX

Numbers in italics refer to pages on which illustrations occur.